MAX

THE MIRACLE DOG

T0054418

MAX

THE MIRACLE DOG

The Heart-Warming Tale of
a Life-Saving Friendship

KERRY IRVING

with Matt Whyman

HarperElement
An imprint of HarperCollins*Publishers*
1 London Bridge Street
London SE1 9GF

www.harpercollins.co.uk
Macken House, 39/40 Mayor Street Upper,
Dublin 1, D01 C9W8, Ireland

First published by HarperElement 2020
This paperback edition published 2020

11

Photographs courtesy of the author with the following exception:
page 8 Andy Commins/Daily Mirror/PA Archive/PA Images

Kerry Irving asserts the moral right to be
identified as the author of this work

A catalogue record of this book is
available from the British Library

ISBN 978-0-00-835352-0

Printed and Bound in the UK using 100% Renewable Electricity at
CPI Group (UK) Ltd

MIX
Paper | Supporting
responsible forestry
FSC
www.fsc.org   FSC™ C007454

This book is produced from independently certified FSC™ paper
to ensure responsible forest management.

For more information visit: www.harpercollins.co.uk/green

This book is dedicated to all the animals
who have ever helped a human.

They walk beside us when we
are beside ourselves.

Contents

Part Three

Prologue

'ARE YOU READY, MAX? *If anyone's going to help me do this, it's you.'*

The dog sitting at my side looks up and meets my gaze. His tail swishes back and forth across the ground, sweeping pine needles aside. Behind us is the little tent we've just slept in overnight in preparation for this day. In the distance, beyond the forests, crested by snow and looming high against the dawn sky, stands a rocky summit that I hope to conquer.

Once upon a time, the prospect of hiking up Ben Nevis would be something I'd just take in my stride. People from all around the world come to this pocket of Scotland to follow the path to the top. Today, it represents something so much more than Britain's highest mountain. For me, this is a challenge that until recently I'd have considered impossible. It is, I believe, a chance for me to face my fears.

If it wasn't for Max, in fact, I wouldn't be here at all.

'Let's go,' I say, and so we begin our walk.

We're up so early, there's nobody else around. Early bars of sunshine push through the forest and fall across the path. Max trots ahead, nose to the ground and with his shoulders moving like pistons, before circling back around with an eye on me. He's such a watchful dog. It's characteristic of his breed, but there's something special about this Springer Spaniel. Nobody understands me better than Max, or knows the sense of trepidation in my mind as we negotiate a stile and begin the challenge that could make or break me. Alone, it would be very easy for me to just turn around now, head home and say, 'Yeah, it's amazing at the top!' and nobody would be any the wiser. With Max here, I'm reminded that I'd only be fooling myself.

I decided to leave at this time for two reasons. Moving at my pace, it's going to take a lot longer than most for us to reach the very top. Every step I take requires care and consideration, while I'm constantly braced for a jolt of pain that could stop me dead. We're following the pony track, which is also known as the tourist route. By mid-morning, I could expect the path that begins to zigzag across the mountain's lower flanks to fill with hikers and that's the main reason why I've set out so early. I don't want anyone to see me but my dog. Right now, the last thing I need is for some 75-year-old carrying a big rucksack to go bounding past and then wonder what's keeping a seemingly fit man in his forties from going at the same pace. Part of the problem, I always think, is that I look fine from the outside. In reality, I have to watch every footstep because one slip could lead to searing pain.

It's hard for me to relax, but I never feel under pressure from Max to move faster. He's off the lead and investigating the path as if to check it's safe for me. He's never been the kind of dog to race off, into a world of his own, or to leave me feeling as if I'm holding him up. Nor does he stick so rigidly at my side that I risk tripping over him. That's not what makes him tick and one of many reasons why we've bonded this closely. He gives me space to breathe along with the sense that I'm not alone.

Max is here for me, just as I'm here for him. We're doing this together because only he understands that if it all goes wrong then I tried my very best. If I'm going to fail, I'll do so with just Max. He's my little friend, my constant companion and guardian angel rolled into one frequently muddy, slightly smelly Spaniel.

We pick our way up the path, clambering over loose stone and steps cut into the hillside. I stop frequently just so I can get my breath and also to enjoy the view. This is something I have thought about doing for some time and it's hard to believe I'm actually here. As the sun is only just climbing into the sky the temperature is perfect. It's a crystal-clear day, with a freshening breeze that stiffens up as we go. I have supplies for us both, but right now, Max is focused on not dropping his stick. He's just picked it up from a gulley and I can be sure he'll carry it all the way to the top and back down again. Once he commits to something, he never gives up and I remind myself of this as I battle my misgivings about coming so far.

It had taken us over half a day to drive here from my home in the Lake District. The journey turned out to be torturous for me. It was probably the furthest I'd gone since my life changed so dramatically several years previously. Behind the wheel, I found that everything from braking to turning caused shooting pains to travel from my neck and radiate through my back and arms. Max travelled up front in the passenger seat beside me. It's where he chooses to sit and I love having him by my side – especially during testing times.

Despite hours of discomfort on the road, I was excited about the trip. It's all about my dog and me. A boys' weekend away. It was only after we arrived at the campsite, and I had put up the tent, that the effort of just getting here caught up with me. All I wanted to do was sleep. It was the first time that Max had spent a night under canvas, however. I wasn't even sure he'd settle. He sniffed around while I laid out my sleeping bag and his blanket. Then I invited him inside.

Max slipped in without hesitation, curled up as if this was where he belonged, and that was that.

We spent the next day just enjoying short walks through the woodland at the foot of the mountain. I needed to rest, recover my strength and prepare for the climb. I didn't sleep much overnight, but once we had set off and left the pine trees behind us I found that my reservations about this hike started to lift. We have quite a distance to go, but Max isn't just here for the fresh air, sights and sounds. He's a comforting presence, content for me to move at my own pace and with something in those long looks he gives me that says: 'I'm here for you.'

Ben Nevis is one of those mountains you can't truly appreciate from a picture. It's only when you're here, looking up at the summit, that you think: 'Wow, that's pretty big!' It's a fair distance to the top and not the easiest hike.

I had studied the map, only to discover that the path had been redirected due to erosion. It means I have to follow a bigger loop and I'm not prepared for that. I have to keep stopping from about a third of the way up to loosen my shoulders. This is down to the fact that I've been tensing my body as I walk, fearful one wrong footing would drop me to the ground in agony. At one point, where the path cuts around an outcrop, I stop and lean against it just to shake out the tension. Max is at my side immediately, looking up at me as the breeze ruffles his long ears.

'I'm not giving up,' I assure him. 'Have faith, we can do this.'

The terrain begins to change as we climb higher. For one thing, the steps become bigger and more testing. So, one minute I'm walking normally and the next I'm forced out of my comfort zone as I grab at grass clumps and rocks to haul myself upwards. That's when it starts to kick in what a big deal this is for me. At the same time, we've reached a point where I can look out across lochs and tarns at a seemingly infinite horizon. It makes me realise how far we've climbed and that there can be no stopping us now.

When we reach the mountain's snowline, Max switches into a different gear. He loves the snow and as he hasn't seen any since the winter, it's a chance to come into his own as a Springer Spaniel by leaping into the drifts. It makes me smile to watch him bounding, his paws sinking into the powdery drifts, and though I can hardly follow suit, it's enough to push me onwards.

Shortly afterwards, with one of my regular checks to see how far we've come, I spot a figure striding towards us.

He's a long way down, but moving so much faster than anything I could manage, and that focuses my attention. I'm happy being alone with Max, but having set off so early, I've got it into my head that I could be the first to reach the summit that day. I'm hardly the first to try conquering Ben Nevis, but just then I feel like a pioneer and I don't want anyone to get there before me.

'Let's push on,' I say, and not just to Max.

We don't have much further to climb, but the hiker continues to close the gap. I try not to panic, or overreach myself, because the last thing I want this far from help is to find myself locked up in agony. To focus, I kept my gaze trained on Max. I remind myself just where this began, at a point in my life that could not get any lower, and how close we are to reaching a high.

Towards the summit, the path opens up onto a stony plateau. It's bitterly cold at this height, much of which is down to the wind chill, and so I'm glad that I've come out in my extreme weather hiking gear. With my eyes smarting, I sight the famous cairn a short distance ahead: a 10-foot pillar of stones that also serves as a trig point to help climbers and hikers orientate themselves. It also marks the very top of Ben Nevis. My heart begins to gallop. I check over my shoulder once again. The hiker is now close enough for me to determine it's a young man, and yet despite his brisk pace there's no way now that he can overtake me.

'Max,' I declare, and he registers my voice immediately, 'we made it.'

I lay my hand on the cairn with Max at my side and my eyes brimming with tears. What had seemed all but unthinkable to me only recently has become a reality. We have scaled well over 1,300 metres from the campsite to be here. It's taken us three and a half hours and I stand upon that summit a changed man, someone who could do anything from this moment on. I feel elated, relieved, and with so much love for my loyal little friend.

'Well done!' The voice behind me catches me by surprise. I turn to face the hiker who had been closing in on us. He beams broadly and reaches down to ruffle Max's head.

'Congratulations to you, too,' I say, and smile cheekily at him. 'You're the second person on the summit today. The third if you include my dog.'

The hiker, a tourist from Germany, laughs and shakes my hand. We chat for a couple of minutes before he sets off to take in the view from the other side of the plateau. I am quite content to sit against the cairn, out of the wind, and just relish this moment. From my pack, I fish out a drinking bowl for Max and a thermos of water for us to share, along with some treats to mark our achievement. I let Max enjoy the gravy bones while I eat a slice of malt loaf. I had packed a banana in an outside pocket of my pack, but it turns out it's frozen solid. I don't keep my gloves off for long.

It's too cold to stay at the summit for more than a few minutes. Before we leave, however, I have one final thing to do. Even before I press the phone to my ear I have tears in my eyes once again. After everything we've been through, my emotions are never far from the surface.

'Ange?' I say when my wife answers my call. 'It's me, Kerry. We've done it!'

'Done what?' she says after a pause and then seems to remind herself. 'Oh, the climb.'

'We're at the top! Ben Nevis! Max and me, we made it all the way.'

'Well, that's nice,' she says cheerily and I know just what this means. Angela works as a hairdresser from home. Her friendly but formal tone tells me she has a customer with her just then. Alone, she wouldn't hold back like this. I smile to myself, tell her I love her and will call again when we reach the campsite. 'Yes, that would be great,' she says to sign off. 'Thanks very much! I'll see you soon.'

I stow my phone while grinning at Max. It feels like he knows just what's going on at home as well. Then I rise carefully to my feet and look around one final time. With magnificent views across the rugged wilderness below, I feel like a king of the world and so proud to have Max alongside me. I hope he shares my sense of achievement for in recent times we have both come such a long way.

'Let's roll,' I say, because this isn't the end of our journey. With Max at my side, it's just the beginning.

Part One

1

A Boy on the Beach

MY HOME IS IN THE LAKE DISTRICT, and also my heart. It's where I belong, and that feeling of being rooted is so important to me. The rugged landscape is where I am happiest. It's also seen me at a desperate low point in my life, and where I met a very special dog who changed everything. The fells shape the backdrop to the story of Max and me, along with majestic expanses of water that reflect the sky above, and yet my earliest memories aren't from here. Those were formed far from the northwest of England, in a small coastal town called Fish Hoek on South Africa's Cape Peninsula.

I was born in Shropshire, the youngest of three boys. I have never known why we were there when I arrived. We just didn't stay for long enough to set down any kind of roots. My dad was a naval engineer. He spent a great deal of time at sea. Soon after my arrival in the early sixties he was posted abroad. Rather than stay behind, my mum packed up our belongings and we took the long trip by boat to start a new life halfway around the globe. As a family, we went on to spend five happy years in a world of our own.

The one thing I remember most about that time is the beach. The sand was the colour of bleached bone, backed by a string of pastel-painted beach huts overlooking a boundless blue bay. I learned to crawl and walk there, and splash about it in the surf under supervision from my mum. Sharks patrolled the waters around the cape, so she never let me stray. During the heat of the day, we took to the shade and drank sugar cane water. At low tide, I developed a fascination for picking over rock pools in search of crabs. Sometimes I would test my parents by smuggling home my new crustacean friends in a bucket for a sleepover under my bed.

When I think back to those formative years, it's really just a melting pot of images, sounds, tastes and smells, from the giant clouds that would cluster over the mountain ranges to the sea salt on my skin. There is no narrative in my mind. I just remember it to be a safe and pleasant time, with no sense that everything was set to change.

We returned to the UK when my father's navy service came to an end after years of working on ships in dock and at sea, but by then my parents felt it was time to move on. Both my mum and dad come from Penrith, a small market town just east of the Lakes in Cumbria's Eden Valley, and so they decided to return to their roots.

Despite leaving a job he loved, my dad's years of experience earned him solid employment in the area as a service engineer for a washing-machine manufacturer. That afforded us a nice house in a little terrace under the railway bridge within view of open countryside and the distant trace of the fells beyond. Best of all, for a lad my age, was the fact that we were just a stone's throw from a farm. I loved to visit the animals. I was enamoured by the pigs and the chickens. I'd ask my older brothers if they would take me, but more often than not they'd each be doing their own thing. They didn't dislike me, I was just too young for them. So, when they took off without me, I would drift down the track to the farm gate to see my livestock friends. I was quite happy on my own, I always have been. You could say that was the beginning of my life as a loner, but at the time I didn't see it that way. In fact, once that little boy made it through the farm gate, he found himself in good company.

Talking to the animals seemed like the most natural thing in the world to me. Yes, it's what kids do, but I've never grown out of it! There's something magical when you know they're listening. It's a connection, and we all need those in life. More than anything, however, I loved to be outdoors. I liked the birdsong and the breeze on my face and the sense that I could go anywhere. I was happy in my own company; the kind of boy who could pick up a stick and transform it into a sword in my imagination, or create a den from branches and ferns and turn it into a castle. I was also oblivious to any sense of danger. I liked to play down by the river, where the current could pick up forcefully whenever rainwater drained off the hills. Even the abandoned steam train line was another good draw for me. It had once been the main connection between Penrith and Keswick in the Lakes. In those days, the stoker on board the train would discard lumps of coal onto the side of the track if they were too big for the firebox. Knowing that I liked to spend time there, my dad would even send me down with a bucket to pick up what I could find for the fire.

While I felt at home outside, life inside seemed increasingly uncomfortable. I would come back to find an air of tension between my parents. I was too young to understand what had come between them; I just knew something wasn't right.

To bring us together, my dad came home one day with a Collie. We called him Rex, which was almost compulsory as a dog name in those days. I was too young to think of Rex as my dog. Still, I considered him to be one of the family. I used to take him for walks across the fields – I think we both got cabin fever quite quickly inside the house, and so it was a good excuse to get out for a short while. I didn't feel as if I was in charge, watching him run and gambol through the grass and the reed beds. It just seemed like we were equals in the world.

We also took on a cat, but my father didn't get on with it at all. I suspect the feeling was mutual, because the cat always made himself scarce whenever he was around. Even so, my dad considered him to be a nuisance we didn't need. One morning, I was told the cat had gone to live on a farm across town. I remember listening to my father explain his absence while wondering what had caused the livid scratches on his forearms. Who knows? It may well be that the innocence of childhood protected me from the whole story, which was certainly the case when it came to the state of my parents' marriage.

2

End of an Idyll

'GET OUT! And don't come back!'

When my dad shoved my mum from the house, I just stood and watched in shock. A shouting match had broken out just moments earlier, which was so intense that neither of them seemed to register that I was in the kitchen with them.

'Stop, Dad!' I cried, but he was too busy blocking the door with his shoulder as my mum fought to get back in. 'Stop it!'

Whatever had caused them to go to war like this, I was caught in the middle. I had never seen Dad this furious before, while Mum screamed and hammered on the door so forcefully I wanted to cover my ears.

'Give me my boys!' she yelled. 'Kerry!'

I tried to pull my dad away, but I was only little and had never felt so useless. Mum even tried to climb in through the kitchen window, but he just pushed her back.

'Mum!' I cried hysterically, 'I want Mum!'

It was a fight I will never forget, and one that saw my parents' marriage end in wreckage. Mum moved out that day and took me with her, while my two brothers stayed with Dad. There was no negotiation or calm conversation, I just threw myself on Mum at the first opportunity while Dad just vowed that it was over between them.

With a suitcase packed in a hurry, we went to stay with her parents in Penrith. They were old school about marriage, and failed to understand why she and my dad could even consider separating as an option. Still, they took us in. When my mum stopped crying she kept telling me that she loved me and that everything would be okay. I was barely eight years old, however I had seen and heard things that just undermined my place in the world. I'd spent more of my life in South Africa than here, and now that happy boy on the beach had all but disappeared into the past. At such a young age I just struggled to process what was going on. On the one hand I was told not to worry, and on the other, it was just there under the surface all the time.

The fight I had witnessed turned out to be the opening conflict in a horrible, messy divorce. As children, we became weapons in a war. What's more, my older brothers resented the fact somehow I managed to stay with Mum and left them behind. They just made me feel guilty when I saw them, as if I had let them down. At the same time, life at my grandparents' house wasn't easy. While I felt deeply unsettled at being uprooted without warning, my grandmother had Parkinson's disease. I had no understanding of what that meant, of course. I just saw the symptoms: the tremors, sense of detachment and the slowness of movement, and with no explanation, she scared me. I couldn't relax in the house, fearing she might creep in at any moment. We were also some distance from the countryside. Living in a built-up area just wasn't the same. At times when I needed space, I had nowhere to go.

The only saving grace was my grandfather and his outside interests. He had an allotment nearby, which was his pride and joy. While he had spent most of his life in my grandmother's shadow, he came into his own with a spade in his hand, and I found his knowledge mesmerising. He showed me how to grow vegetables from seed in his greenhouse, plant them out at the right time and care for them as they grew. In summer, we'd sit outside to eat tomatoes picked straight from the vine. I'd make a complete mess of mine, but the taste and that fresh, tangy aroma was bewitching. My grandfather also loved to play lawn bowls. He spent a lot of time at the club opposite the railway station in Penrith. I have fond memories of just watching a game shape up and feeling like I was on his team. He was a really good player as well. When he died some years later, his ashes were scattered on the green there.

As well as my grandfather's allotment, the bowling club became another place where I could go to escape from the house. It also took my mind off the sense of longing I felt every time I thought about my brothers and my dad. Mum was doing her very best for me, of course, but with the divorce going through, she had her issues. It was just a confusing time. If I went back, Dad would try to score points against Mum, and she would do the same when I returned. Over time, the relationship between them just broke down completely, while my brothers continued to give me a hard time about living apart from them. I felt I had to make it up to them somehow and badgered them to help me find parts for a big go-kart we used to play with in Cape Town. It had been shipped back in several sea chests, but bits had gone missing en route. They didn't want to know, much to my dismay, and yet all I wanted was to fix things.

'Mum,' I said one day, and it took me all the courage I could muster, 'I want to be with my brothers.'

Quietly, on the inside, I imagined hearing this from her youngest son must have broken her. But from where I was sitting across from her at supper one day, she offered me a brave smile and then promised she'd see what could be done. In reality, as my parents had stopped speaking to each other, they couldn't come close to an amicable agreement. The matter was dragged into the divorce proceedings and ended up going to court. It meant I had to sit in stuffy side rooms with solicitors and a panel of strange people asking me questions about who I wanted to live with.

By now, it was clear that my mum didn't want me to leave her. That made it so hard for me to speak up and say that's what I wanted to do. I felt like I was letting her down, but they asked me to be honest and so I did as I was told. There was no way I could make everyone happy; all I could do was be truthful and the hard fact was that I felt miserable away from my brothers. In lots of ways, when the court made the decision for me to rejoin them, it just made things so much worse between my parents. I moved back to the terrace, and while I found more life there, my mum didn't like it all. She started accusing Dad of manipulating me behind her back, and he lashed out in return with similar force. They would talk badly about each other to me, and I just found it confusing and upsetting.

I was a primary school kid and the two people who were supposed to take care of me were at war with each other. All trust between them had completely broken down and I was caught in the middle. I had wanted to be with my brothers, but frankly, they were rarely at home. I couldn't blame them, given the way Dad spoke about Mum. In fact, soon after I moved back, my older brother fell out with him. He left to join our mother, before turning 18 shortly after that and striking out on his own. Surrounded by upset and conflict, I found myself back in a world of my own with Rex and the farm animals for company and adventures to be had across the countryside trails.

Despite the turbulence that engulfed my parents, we did have what seemed like good times. At the end of the week, Dad would come home from work and take us all out to the pub with him. He'd pick us up in his transit van and we'd drive out for the evening. We were too young to join him at the bar. Instead, we'd wait inside the van or in the beer garden and he would bring us a shandy each and a packet of salt and vinegar crisps. It felt like a treat, even if we had effectively been left to our own devices. In my eyes, it was a taste of normal family life. What we didn't begin to recognise, until one evening when a roadside breathalyser tested positive, was that our dad had a drinking problem.

It happened one evening during the week. Dad was on a call-out to service an appliance at a big hotel overlooking Ullswater. On the spur of the moment, he'd decided to take my middle brother and me with him. All day, a storm had been brewing, and as daylight faded on the drive out, so the wind picked up and the rain came down. From the lake road, we looked out across a body of water that looked like hammered metal. Normally, accompanying our father on a job like this, we'd have played down by the shore. By the time he had parked and scuttled into the hotel with his toolkit, the storm was so intense that it felt like we were under siege.

My brother had bagged the front bench. I was just sitting amongst all the electrical junk in the back, which wasn't much fun at all. Bored and fractious, we bickered about cracking open the windows to stop the van from steaming up. Over an hour later, when Dad finally hurried out of the darkness with his collar turned up against the downpour, he was quick to bellow at us to behave. I don't know whether he'd been offered a drink on the job or had brought his own supplies. Either way, he shouldn't have slotted the key into the ignition, fired up the engine and the headlights, and set off back along the lake road. It was a bumpy ride in the back at the best of times. That night, as the wipers struggled to maintain a clear view ahead, I found myself sliding around as if we were at sea.

'Dad,' I appealed to him at one point as we followed a bend just a little too quickly for my liking.

Sliding this way and that, but restrained by his seat belt, my brother giggled to himself. Without that luxury, I failed to see the funny side.

'It's the weather,' our father reasoned, as if that was to blame for his driving, and then scolded my brother for laughing.

I didn't dare say any more after that. With just the glow from the dashboard to cut through the darkness, I anchored myself as best I could in the back. Every time we cut through standing water on the road it would crash against the chassis, which my father sought to drown out by cranking up a song on the radio. The crooning sounded completely at odds with the ferocity of the storm. It was all I could hear, in fact. Minutes later, when the van skipped onto two wheels and then left the road, my first thought was that a bolt of lightning had struck us. The noise was deafening, from scraping metal to fragmenting glass, while the vehicle rotated onto its roof and then by another 90 degrees like a sticking drum in one of my dad's machines.

When the van came to rest in the road, with the radio still playing but a sense that the world had tipped onto its side, Dad was quick to call out to us both. Shaken and bruised, and miraculously spared from serious injury, we crawled out of the wreckage in turn. I was last to make my way through the buckled frame where the windscreen had once been. As I did so, I picked out the rear-view mirror that had been smashed from its moorings. Dad reached in to help me out. As my brother sobbed behind him, all I could see were scratches and concern on his face. I showed them the mirror, shocked to the core but desperate for everything to be alright.

'This will look great on our go-kart,' I declared.

3

Hard Times

THE ACCIDENT RESULTED IN A DRIVING BAN for my father. More immediately, such a narrow escape for us all shook our family to the core. Sadly, it didn't bring my parents any closer. As soon as Mum learned what had happened, she went straight to court and contested that our dad wasn't fit to look after us. Until that moment, my middle brother and I had never once questioned whether our father's drinking was an issue. At the hearing, our mother claimed it was more than an isolated incident. From that moment on, I started looking at my dad in a different light whenever he had a beer, which seemed to be more frequently at home after he lost his licence.

Mum also had other pressing reasons to have us back. Shortly after the accident, my dad started seeing a woman from the local shoe repairers, who would quickly become our stepmother. Through my mother's eyes, her arrival in his life saw us sidelined. We were frequently left to feed ourselves and wore dirty school uniforms held together with safety pins. At the same time, whenever we saw her, Mum stopped being a shadow of her former self and began to sparkle once again. It wasn't long before she introduced me to the man who would become my stepfather. He seemed nice, and clearly made her happy, so that was alright by me. As the relationship duly developed, they even found a place to live together in Penrith. It all helped her case when she argued that her boys would be better off living with her.

So, along with my middle brother, I went back to live with our mother. Once the divorce came through and Mum remarried, it really did seem as if she was creating a new chapter in our lives. In some ways it was a honeymoon period for us all. Had I been a little older, I would have known that it would always come to an end.

If my stepfather resented the fact that his new wife came with kids as part of the package, he didn't keep it to himself for long. After a short time, it became clear to my middle brother and me that this new family figurehead considered us to be a nuisance. To begin with, he would fall silent in our presence, as if we were interrupting something, which just made us feel uncomfortable. It didn't get any worse than that when my mother, who was just too enamoured with him to notice, was around. She worked in a restaurant, often through the evenings. That's when things really began to change. Alone in the house with us, my stepfather made no attempt to hide his true feelings. When he didn't just blank us completely, or mutter that we were in his way, he'd launch into profanities about our dad. It was as if he regarded him as responsible for the fact that his new life with our mother was weighed down by her boys. I couldn't blame my middle brother when he turned 16, left school and announced that he was moving out. He'd found a live-in job at a hotel, which left me alone with a man who openly despised me.

'You're a good-for-nothing bastard, Irving,' he would mutter, like my surname was some kind of curse.

Then came the house rules. My stepfather just seemed to introduce them at will in a bid to contain me. I wasn't allowed to switch on the lights unless he was in the room because I'd be wasting his money. In the same way, the television was a luxury only he could afford. Come winter time, lighting the fire to keep warm was out of the question. If my stepfather was chilly, however, then he'd demand to know why I hadn't got it going and then reprimand me until the house was an acceptable temperature. Life revolved around him alright. If he tolerated me under the same roof as him by the thinnest of margins, then it was on a seen-but-not-heard basis. Any kind of noise I made, from scraping a chair to sit down or causing the stairs to creak as I crept upstairs, would earn me a tongue-lashing. The control he exerted became increasingly stifling. It reached the point where I practically couldn't even breathe in his presence. In short, it felt as if the sole purpose of his existence was to make me feel as unwelcome in his house as possible.

As a boy approaching his teenage years, all this affected me greatly. Inside the house, feeling like I didn't belong and constantly on edge in case my stepfather turned against me, all I could do was go to a place in my head that shut it all down. As a result, I just took every opportunity to stay away. As long as I obeyed his evening curfew, and was home before eight o'clock without fail, I spent as much time outside as I could.

One year, my grandfather from Penrith presented me with a bike. I don't know if he had a sense of how things were for me at home, but I leapt upon it as a chance to get away. The Raleigh Arena was a racer with drop handlebars. In those days it was popular with kids as a first grown-up bike, and I loved the freedom it gave me. I had learned to get away on foot from an early age, but this changed everything. No matter how bad things got at home, I could climb onto the saddle and pedal my way as far away as possible. To begin with, before I found my riding confidence, I would head for the paths around the school playing field and ride around the perimeter. Sometimes the caretaker would come chasing after me, which just made me all the more determined to keep going. Anything but break away and head back home before I was ready. I imagine I drove the poor man to distraction! He only got a break as I became more adventurous and took myself further afield. I probably only went a couple of miles, but to a young lad feeling this trapped, I felt like a bird with wings.

For some kids with troubled backgrounds, school can become a sanctuary. I wanted it to feel like a place of safety, somewhere I could be myself, but if it was raining on a school day, my stepfather would refuse to take me. As I plodded through the puddles, he didn't even glance in my direction if he happened to pass. I'd just watch his car drive on by, so I suppose it's no surprise that I struggled to fit in when I got there. It was tough, I think, to switch off the defences I had built to survive at home. In general, I just kept my own company and had a very small circle of friends. Even then it was a struggle to find common ground. Sometimes they would come into school talking about programmes they had all watched the evening before, like *Grange Hill* or *Mork & Mindy*, and all I could do was nod along and try not to feel left out. They knew about my stepfather and his treatment of me. But then if I ever dared bring anyone home, he might choose to be really nice. Much depended on his view of their intelligence. Having left school at 11, my stepfather basically regarded people who showed a hint of wit or brains as being a legitimate target for his scorn and condescension. If he deemed them to be unthreatening in that respect then he'd crack a joke with them, usually at my expense. He could even be funny and they would laugh. In a way that made it worse because they'd wonder what my problem was with him.

As the years ticked by, my stepfather continued his campaign of venom towards me. A couple of years after I started secondary school, though, my mother was given a puppy called Prince by my uncle. Prince was a black and white Sprocker, which is a mix between a Springer and Cocker Spaniel. It was great to have a dog again and finally have a fun, joyful companion. I would take Prince out on walks, and attempted to train him to sit, fetch, lie down and roll over. He was a smart dog, and my first introduction to the Spaniel breed. Alone with Prince, there was just something about the look he would give me that made me feel special. He depended on me for guidance, even if it was just a glance back at a fork in the woodland path to see which way I planned to turn. Nobody had ever turned to me like that before. On walks, it gave me a sense of purpose, and also a familiarity with dogs that would stay with me throughout my life.

I could never let on how involved I was with Prince. Had my stepfather found out, he would've got rid of him in the blink of an eye. In some ways, I came to consider Prince to be the heart of my family in that home. He didn't judge me or make me feel bad, and while our mother always watched out for me, she just wasn't aware of the bigger picture. She knew my stepfather could be difficult with me, but had no idea what he could be like when her back was turned.

Quite simply, every second under the same roof as my stepfather left me feeling isolated and inadequate. I just couldn't tell Mum. He was just too important to her, after everything she had been through, though I failed to understand what she saw in him. Then again, it wasn't all sweetness and light between them. When they fell out, they did so dramatically and made a poor attempt to hide it from us. Sometimes I would listen to their rows from my bedroom and silently urge her to leave him. Once or twice I even heard her scream at him that they would be better off apart. I just crossed my fingers, squeezed my eyes shut and hoped that she would appear at my door at any moment and ask me to pack my bags. Instead, whenever she did come to check on me, she'd observe that it looked like I was carrying the weight of the world on my shoulders.

'What's wrong?' she would sometimes ask, whenever life with my stepfather became too much. 'Why won't you talk to me?'

I wanted to feel close to Mum, but never opened up to her about anything. Over time, I just learned to shut away difficult thoughts and feelings, and that's how I felt safe. Besides, I had already broken her heart once. I was only young when I told her that I wanted to be with my brothers. This time I knew what revealing my stepfather's true nature would do to her.

'I'm fine,' I would say instead. 'It's nothing.'

Through the years, many times I tried to tell my dad what life was like back home. I didn't feel any need to put my worries into words, I just saw him as someone who might intervene. He didn't get on with my stepfather, but when I hinted all was not well, he just told me to stay out of his way. I was disappointed, but also aware that Dad had issues of his own. Having rolled the van, his relationship with drinking slowly spilled into the light. Eventually, it became quite clear to me that he had a problem with alcohol. What's more, he was one of those drinkers who becomes unapproachable when intoxicated. It also brought out an angry, impatient and sometimes violent streak in him.

Whenever I went to stay with my father and his new wife, I found myself living under threat of the belt. I didn't have to step far out of line for him to reach for it, and my stepmother never stopped him. Sometimes, I could spend all day out in the woods and fields. I'd only go home for lunch if I knew that they were out for the day. Despite everything going on behind closed doors, I look upon that time in the wild with great fondness. I got up to all sorts, often on my own or sometimes with local kids from the farms. I learned to shoot air rifles and lit more campfires than I've had hot dinners. It's a wonder I didn't come to any harm, but frankly, it was safer than being in the house.

By the time I turned 16, I found myself gearing up to face the world as if I was wearing an invisible suit of armour. From the outside, I looked like I could take care of myself. On the inside, where nobody could see me, I was a lonely and insecure young man with little self-confidence. I was desperate to get away from my stepfather and leave my dad to his drinking habit. I just didn't want to leave an area I had grown to love. Because outside the two suffocating houses I was supposed to consider home, the fells, lakes, trails and valleys of the Northwest were where I could breathe freely.

From the moment I set off with Max from the campsite at the foot of Ben Nevis, my focus was on reaching the summit. As a physical challenge, it was down to me to keep putting one walking boot in front of the other. As a leap of faith, however, I just focused on my dog in the belief that he would lead me there.

'We did it!' I say to Max as much as myself when we finally stand upon that highest point and look out towards the horizon. It seems hard to believe we are really here. It's something I have thought about constantly since making the decision for us to come here – something that would have been unthinkable before I met Max. 'We did it after everything we've been through.'

Conquering Ben Nevis is a milestone for any hiker. The German who joined us shortly after our arrival at the top looked thrilled to be there. Even so, he had no idea what a momentous achievement this was for us both. Having swapped pleasantries and taken photos, and also called my wife at work, I turn my attention to the descent. Looking at Max, who is busy exploring the scree, only one of us is feeling the effects of the climb. Even so, I can't think it will be as challenging to make our way back down.

Within minutes of setting out, I realise how drastically I have underestimated the challenge.

When you're living in constant pain, and then become tired and fatigued, that pain becomes much harder to manage. As Max and I make our way off the top, I have to think hard about every placement of my lead foot. I can't afford to slip or slide. One false move would cause white-hot pain to shoot up my spine to my neck, and I know that could drop me to the ground in agony. Within a short space of time, exhausted by the efforts of the day, I begin to catch myself on the cusp of making mistakes. Instead of being loose and free, and able to react to any slip before it catches up with me, I just tense my body as if braced for the worst. As a result, with my footing becoming heavier, I sense the muscles in my neck go into spasm. Pain radiates into my jawline, which is excruciating. All I want to do now is get off that mountain, but there is no shortcut. It's just me, my dog, and a sense of sheer determination.

At times, where the path became too steep or technical, I have to turn and shuffle down on my hands and knees. I even slide a few yards on my backside. Max keeps a close eye on me throughout. He doesn't wander off, or lose himself to a noise or smell. Every time I look around for my dog, I find his watchful expression that has become so important to me as well as that blessed stick clamped between his jaws!

'I'm sorry,' I say, aware that he could probably race down this mountainside in no time at all. 'If I make it to the campsite in one piece, I promise you an ice cream at the earliest opportunity.'

I smile to myself. Max may not understand, but that dog has a taste for a vanilla scoop like no other.

As the gradient becomes less challenging, we begin to pass people on their way up. Some are dressed in mountaineering gear, others have set out in deck shoes and board shorts. It's a mixed bag of ability and age, but it lifts my spirits whenever we pass anyone. They probably wonder why a man in his forties is moving like a geriatric, with what they must assume is an assistance dog at his side. All I know is that Max and I have achieved something that would have been impossible for me only a short time ago. So, despite the odd look of concern, I come down that mountain carrying a huge sense of pride.

By the time we clamber back over the stile and clear the forest path to the campsite, that pride has transformed into euphoria. My cheeks are wet with tears as we pass through the entrance. Rather than head for our pitch, I steer Max towards the river so we can cool off. If it had been bracingly fresh at the summit, the heat of the day has pooled at ground level. What's more, if there's one thing Max likes in this world more than anything else, that's the chance to get wet.

Minutes later, having coaxed the stick from Max, I watch him launch after it from the bank, his tail rotating in excite-

ment. All I can do is shield myself from the splash, cheer, clap and recognise that without this dog, I wouldn't be here at all. As I gingerly follow my best friend into the river, I realise I am lucky to be alive to enjoy such simple pleasures that make this life so precious.

4

Into the Wild

ONE DAY, WHEN I WAS 13, my dad summoned me round to his place. It was unusual for him to want to see me beyond agreed visits. Even when I did spend time there, his only interest wasn't in talking to me, but mocking my step-dad. I just knew that something was up.

'I'm moving away,' he told me soon after I arrived, and placed his arm around my stepmother. 'We're emigrating to Australia.'

'Oh,' was all I could say in response. 'Right.'

I felt no sense of elation or relief that this would spell an end to being fearful of my own father. Just then, I wasn't particularly sorry to see him go either. After years of putting up barriers so I couldn't be hurt, I just looked at him blankly. I nodded as he explained that life just hadn't been the same since rolling the van, but felt nothing at all.

'We'll be having a going away party,' he said, like this would make everything better. 'I hope you can join us.'

* * *

Once the news had sunk in, I did start to think that I would miss him. I associated the outbursts of anger and the threat of punishment with the smell of alcohol on his breath, but that wasn't a permanent state. When my dad wasn't drinking, I reminded myself, he could be alright. We shared the same sense of humour and at times I felt like he really cared for me. Sober, he could talk to me on a level, as if he recognised that I was no longer a kid. While his older sons were long gone, it struck me that this was his way of making up for lost time. In fact, as he made preparations to pack up and begin a new life, he began to look ahead with me in mind.

'One day, perhaps you can join me,' he said. 'I'll have a business up and running. We can work together and when I'm gone, it'll all be yours. Every last penny, son. You can have it all.'

As someone with no clear goals or even a belief that I could be ambitious, this sounded like an invitation I couldn't ignore. Dad stressed that now was not the right time to be taking me with him, and besides, the custody terms prevented any such move halfway across the world. All the same, he made a solemn promise that when the right opportunity presented itself, I could join him on the other side of the world in making this fresh start.

My mum, of course, interpreted his offer very differently. She saw it as a direct provocation, a means of disrespecting all the hard work she had done in raising me. Mum refused outright to let me discuss his proposal with her. In fact, she even forbade me from going to his leaving party. That really upset me. Despite living in fear of my dad for so long,

I wanted to believe that he had changed. Compared to the way I viewed my stepfather, I was always looking for chinks of light in the picture I painted of my dad. He was quite the showman when he wanted to be; he could make people laugh or talk things up to fully engage them. I always held out hope that he could peel away the drinking and the behaviour that went with it like a villain suit he no longer needed. It could be that easy, or so I thought, for him to reveal the man I wished he could be. After the offer he had made, I figured his farewell party would be my chance to restore our relationship as father and son before the time came when we could be together again. By then, however, my mother was so enraged by his decision to just fly away and leave us that her final word on the subject drove a wedge between us.

'You're just like him!' she snapped at me once. 'Good for nothing and useless!'

'Well, maybe I am!' I raged back at her, and I meant it. Not only was I my father's son, I just didn't feel as if I was capable of shining at anything.

By now, my grades had flat-lined. While my brothers had gone to grammar school, I just wasn't good enough to follow in their footsteps. They used to joke and call me thick and I took that to heart. For me, the classroom was a place where I would sit in quiet confusion and simply tune out. Maths was a case in point, and just undermined my self-confidence even further. I enjoyed some lessons, like geography, and looked forward to playing sports like rugby because that meant being part of a team. Even so, as the terms ticked by I came to accept that I would never be academically minded. The only subjects where I showed a glimmer of promise were practical ones like metalwork and woodwork. I found that I was quite good at putting things together, and by extension, taking them apart to see how they worked. I liked breaking things down into component parts, especially if something wasn't working properly. Unfortunately, I never thought to do the same thing to myself, and figure out what was essentially making me so unhappy. Instead, I carried on finding ways to lock in my feelings so that nobody knew what was really going on inside my heart and mind.

As a teenager, it was girls who came close to finding a way in. While I struggled to trust anybody with my emotions, I enjoyed going on dates with someone I liked so that we could get to know each other a bit better. At the same time, it wasn't me who eventually shut down on them; it was my stepfather who ensured that any blossoming romance would be killed off with a single visit to my house. If I invited a girl back for tea, proud as punch that someone would be interested in me, he would basically just blank her completely. Even if we walked in to find him in a good mood, his face would fall as soon as he saw that I had female company. He wouldn't look around, even after I had introduced her or she made efforts to talk to him. I wanted to die of embarrassment. It was as if my stepfather had spotted a chance for me to be happy and killed it stone-dead. As a result, any blossoming romance I might have had with a girl just ended with an excuse to go home early and then a distancing from me because, frankly, my stepfather was toxic.

Over the years, his attitude towards me didn't soften one bit. Even when I was a young man, he still set about threatening and intimidating me in the same way that he did when I was a bewildered little boy. While my dad's propensity to reach for his belt had tapered as I developed, and he'd begun to talk to me rather than tell me off, my stepfather considered my growing physical presence to be a direct threat to his authority. With his ever-tightening rules, constant gripes and threats, he left me feeling as if I was taking up too much space in the house and effectively eating away at the food budget. Being older, and with a little more independence, I just found more reasons to stay out of his orbit, which is where the Army Cadet Force came to my rescue.

I joined up because it was just something a lot of my friends had done. The idea of being out in the fresh air twice a week, toying with rifles and tents, certainly appealed to me. Plus, I thought I might make some new friends. I just hadn't anticipated that it would be so fulfilling. Within a short space of time, I was attending not only to fit in but because I loved every aspect of the experience.

Every session was an opportunity for me to join young people who shared a similar love of being outdoors. We wore the same uniform, so everyone was equal, in a disciplined but fun environment in which the rules were something to respect rather than fear. As cadets, we were given the opportunity to master new skills and supported in this by both leaders and peers. We went on several training exercises and shared experiences that really helped me to come out of my shell.

Quite simply, for the first time in my life I had found a family. It felt like I belonged and was welcomed in that tribe. I suppose I came to appreciate this more than most because it was something I had never truly experienced before. It certainly pointed me towards a career in the army, which I considered seriously for quite a while. What stopped me was the fact that any sense of purpose the cadets gave me just drained away whenever I headed for home.

Without fail, my stepfather would take one look at me breezing back through the door in my uniform and set out to remind me who was in charge. I might have been too noisy coming in, or brought mud in on my boots. One way or another, he would pick a quarrel with me and quickly escalate it. He used to enjoy watching the wrestling on television, with theatrical bouts between fighters with names like Giant Haystacks, Big Daddy and Kid Dynamo. I don't know whether he saw himself in those guys, but given the opportunity, he'd pounce on me. It began when the wrestling was on one time. I had been sitting beside him on the sofa, tuned out from his running commentary about how he could do better, when suddenly he turned his attention to me. It was just play fighting, or so he said, but I didn't like it from the start. Grinning at my protests, as if I'd reached an age where this kind of thing was acceptable, he'd twist my arm behind my back or pin me to the ground as if we were in the ring. Then slowly, over time, his idea of fun and games became a means of putting me in my place.

'Kerry, you're late,' he said one time when I returned home from cadets.

My stepfather was in the front room, his attention turned from whatever he was watching on the box. I had just closed the front door behind me. I was also well aware of the time because my curfew had yet to begin.

'It's not quite eight o'clock,' I said, and that was enough to bring him to his feet.

'Look at you,' he said, sizing me up and down. I was so proud of my cadet uniform, from my boots to my beret. It gave me a sense of identity that had nothing to do with living in this house. 'Army boy.'

The way he levelled his gaze at me made me feel like he had just declared the start of a bout. All of a sudden, I felt quite alone. I glanced into the kitchen and up the stairs: there was no sign or sound of Mum. I guessed they were out on a late walk with Prince. It was just us in the house. The realisation made me want to reach for the door and walk right out again, but it was too late for that.

'What are you watching?' I said, hoping to distract him as I ducked around him for the front room. 'Hey!'

My stepfather grabbed me forcefully by the scruff of my shirt and squared me round to face him.

'Come on!' he bellowed, practically nose to nose. 'Don't they teach you to fight?'

Before I could draw breath to remind him that cadets wasn't about hand-to-hand combat, he had grabbed me in a headlock.

'Get off!' I yelled. 'Leave me alone!'

Trapped under his arm, I felt just as gripped by shock and sheer humiliation. Even though I had grown, he was still bigger than me and just laughed when I struggled. I pleaded with him to let go, only for him to urge me to fight back like a man.

'Do it, Kerry! Prove yourself to me, show me what you're made of!'

If he still considered this to be a lark, I wasn't laughing in any way. I'd had a great evening with the cadets, only to come back to this. If anything, it just trampled on my belief that I could be good enough to join the army. If I couldn't deal with my stepfather, I thought to myself, what use would I be? Then, as I flailed and thrashed around that sense of helplessness in me turned to anger. In that moment, for the first time ever, I'd had enough. All I wanted to do was show him that he couldn't push me about any more. I tried to swing him against the wall, but my stepfather just picked up on it. 'Is this the best you can do? Is it? *Is it?*'

I wanted to lay that bastard on his back, but he simply had me pinned. Bent double, with my head trapped, he shifted his weight from one foot to the other to keep me contained. I gave it one more shot to break free. Then, choking back tears, I submitted. It felt so pointless to me just then, and summed up how I felt about my life.

For the more I struggled, desperate to be free, my stepfather just tightened his grip on me.

5

School of Life

AT 16, I LEFT SCHOOL. I just saw no point in sitting in classrooms feeling 10 steps behind everyone else. At the time, national unemployment levels stood at a record high of three million. In walking out of the school gates for the final time, I was doing little to keep my options open. If anything, I saw it as the only path open to me.

While I had little by way of self-confidence, I wasn't lazy. I wanted to work, if only so I could earn enough money to stand on my own two feet and get away from my stepfather. With no plan to speak of, or faith in my abilities, I headed for the local job centre. It was a grim, desolate experience. I joined a queue, filled in forms, and then sat across from a man who worked his way through my answers like his mind was on other matters. Despite this awful introduction to working life, I left with appointments for two interviews.

The first one took place at a poultry processing plant. The job, I learned, involved plucking feathers from freshly slaughtered chicken carcasses as they swung by suspended from hooks. I may not have known what I wanted to do with my life, but I understood myself well enough to be sure this wasn't for me. The smell of the place was suffocating, the tedium second to none, but above all, I just felt uncomfortable with the fact that the chickens arriving at the plant in crates on the backs of lorries had lived such miserable lives.

I headed for my second interview with similar reservations. It was with a local butcher, who was looking for an apprentice. Before I arrived, having turned my back on the poultry plant, I felt like my world was caving in on itself. Was I good for nothing else but this? I asked myself, on checking my reflection in the shop window. I looked smart, but felt wretched, and during the interview, I felt as if the old butcher was sizing me up like a slab of meat. I could've cried, but kept my composure and looked him in the eye as he told me all about the family business. I did register the fact that he was big on animal welfare. Everything that came into the shop, so he said, was carefully sourced, and that struck a chord with me. I listened with interest, in fact, even though I had already decided that he was just going through the motions with me.

Back home, I told my mum all about my day. She understood about the poultry factory and made us a cup of tea as I brought her up to speed on my chat with the butcher.

'It doesn't sound so bad,' she said, despite the fact that I had been so down about it. 'We'd get free meat for one thing!'

I wasn't sure if she was joking, but we shared a chuckle all the same. I was dreading the return home of my stepfather, who would no doubt find some fault in the way

I'd presented myself and then pick a fight about my prospects.

As it turned out, by the time he appeared I could happily report that I was in full-time employment.

The knock at the front door came soon after the shops on the high street closed for the day.

'Is your boy here?' I heard a familiar voice ask my mother when she opened up. I joined her at the door, and for a moment failed to recognise the old man without his apron and hat. Then he saw me, and beamed. 'There's an apprenticeship waiting for you, Kerry, if you want it?'

I couldn't think of what I had done to impress the butcher. I honestly thought he would have written me off. Just then, any doubts I had about working in the shop evaporated. It was such a rare thing for me to feel valued and so I seized the opportunity. Even better, on arriving for the first day of my apprenticeship, the butcher decided to set me to work in the back room. I had been so worried about standing behind a counter. That would have meant dealing with people and I didn't feel cut out for that at all. Even the thought of greeting a customer made me feel sick. So, it came as a surprise and a huge relief when he asked me to follow him through a door and stationed me at a steel-topped table with a radio for company. There, with a selection of knives in a block, he then set about teaching me the basics of butchery.

In his view, I had the job nobody else in the shop relished. That old butcher worked me hard. He had high standards, too, and I was eager to please him with the quality of my work. So, whenever I made mistakes, I was determined to learn from the experience and made a point of asking for advice as well as appraisal. In many ways, working with knives took me back to my time alone in the woods. I enjoyed the craftsmanship involved. Yes, I was doing all the horrible things that nobody else fancied, but I made it mine. For almost a year, I could tie on my apron for a day's work knowing that I wouldn't get any grief from people around me. There was banter from the butcher and his assistants, of course, and constructive criticism as my apprenticeship progressed, and that was fine by me. Basically, that back room was my kingdom. Then, one Tuesday morning, a member of staff fell sick without cover.

'Kerry, put your whites on and come in the shop today.'

How I froze when the old butcher put his head around the corner to tell me this.

'What?'

'We need help behind the counter.'

'But—'

'But nothing,' he said, cutting across any excuse I might have come up with, and then held my gaze for a moment. He knew this was my comfort zone, but as a business he needed me front of house. 'Just be yourself, Kerry. You're a decent young man, that's good enough for me.'

A few minutes later, I emerged into the main shop with a face as pale as my butcher's coat. Just then, it felt like I was on a front line. Anyone who walked through that door was a threat, it seemed to me. Thanks to years of being made to feel so worthless, I didn't feel equipped to deal with people.

'Are you sure about this?' I asked when the butcher noted that my hands were trembling. 'I don't want to let you down.'

In response, before he could draw breath, the bell above the door signalled the arrival of the day's first customer. A woman entered with a tartan shopping bag on wheels. The butcher greeted her warmly and then shot me a wink.

'How can I help?' I cleared my throat to start again, because my voice sounded tissue-thin. I had expected her to scowl at me, but the woman just smiled and asked for bacon rashers.

It might not seem like much, but for me, that day was a trial by fire. I didn't relax until it was time to flip the sign on the door to signal we were closed. By then, I was exhausted but also elated. I had served a string of customers and found that I enjoyed it. Okay, I was scared, but that fear quickly vanished as soon as I greeted them and received a friendly reply. It helped that the counter formed a physical barrier, a line nobody could cross. All the same, that soon became invisible as I continued to serve. People weren't monsters, as I had led myself to believe. Not everyone was like my stepfather or my dad. Nobody had set out to make me feel small or threaten some kind of punishment. Customers had treated me in the same way that I treated them and I had loved every minute.

That day was supposed to have been a one-off. As I'd made such an impression on the boss, however, he asked me to give it another shot the next day, and the day after that. Within a week, I was dividing my time between my duties in the back room and serving customers at the counter. Just like my introduction to butchery, once I'd overcome my fears I wanted to learn all there was to selling. It wasn't just about being pleasant, but understanding the customer's needs and learning how to meet them. That meant coming out of my shell and connecting with people, and it proved to be the making of me.

During my apprenticeship, and afterwards in what became a secure job for me, I found myself becoming more outward-looking. I had friends and joined them on evenings out in Penrith. Even as a teenager, I was tall and broad for my age. It meant I could drink in pubs and get into local nightclubs long before I turned 18. Going out after work also proved to be a good way to avoid spending any more time than I had to at home. At every opportunity, I tried to avoid my stepfather. Having reached an age where he could no longer impose a curfew, I just stayed out late enough to feel sure that when I crept home, he would be fast asleep.

In effect, I grew up in that butcher's shop, turning from a shy boy to an outgoing young man who finally believed in himself. It wasn't an instant transformation, and what confidence I gained was fragile, but outwardly, I learned how to project myself. I felt ready to make my mark in the world.

When my boss, the old butcher, announced his retirement, I knew it was time to move on. Having gained a reputation in my role, I quickly found a new position in a bigger shop. I had hoped it would provide me with new challenges, but after a short while I realised it wasn't the same. I didn't feel like I belonged as I had at the old place. It no longer seemed like family. Rather than risk a return to feeling unhappy, I took a temporary job as a warehouseman. It earned me enough money to pay my rent, which of course my stepfather insisted on, and to make the most of my evenings out with friends. I would come to drink like the best of them and survive on little sleep. At the same time, I learned to drive. Not only did that give me more independence from home, I found that I loved being out on the road. So, when an opportunity arose to apply for a role as a van driver for the local bakery, I jumped at it.

The job had perks, and not just free doughnuts. With no desire to spend time at home, it was the antisocial hours that appealed to me. I started work at three in the morning, delivering bread to homes and businesses around the region before the world woke up. My shift was also split. So, I'd return home for lunch, knowing my stepfather would be out, and basically, have the place to myself all afternoon. After a nap I'd be back on the road to pick up flour to deliver to the bakery, with enough time after I clocked off to sink a few pints with the lads before the pub shut.

For almost a year, I barely saw the man I had grown to despise. It was something my mum and I never discussed. I would see her from time to time and we got along just fine. I imagine my stepfather was quite content with the fact that I had found a way to avoid him. Even so, it did little to dampen the tension between us on the rare occasions that we were in the house together. One lunchtime, I came home to find he had taken time off work. He looked up from his paper at the kitchen table and his expression just darkened on seeing me.

'Don't they have a canteen at work?' he asked.

By now, we were barely speaking. We could be civil, especially when Mum was around, but just then we were alone except for the dog. Prince was in his basket, looking like he'd prefer to keep out of it.

'I won't be stopping long,' I told him, and headed for the kettle.

'Good to hear.'

'Unbelievable,' I muttered under my breath with my back turned to him.

'What was that?' The sound of my stepfather scraping his chair back to stand brought me round on my heels. I found him glowering at me. The dog whimpered and curled tighter in his basket.

'Nothing,' I said, raising my palms. I didn't want a row – I'd come home for a bite to eat and a chance to unwind after a busy morning in the van. 'Do you want a cup of tea?'

'I want to know what you just said.' My stepfather took a step forward, squaring up to me. 'Speak up!'

Over the years, I had learned to back down quickly from a situation like this. He'd still catch me with the back of his hand, or put me into one of his wrestling holds, but if I was quick, I could get away without too much grief. I was younger than him and also bigger now. This time, trapped between the kitchen counter and my stepfather as he advanced on me, and feeling like I didn't deserve this grief, I stood my ground.

'Don't do this,' I warned as he raised his hand to me.

I caught him by the wrist, only for him to shove me hard. Instinctively, I grabbed his shirt to steady myself and that's how the fight broke out. It was over quicker than I could process, but in that moment, we traded several punches before I put him on his back.

In shock at what had just happened to him, my stepfather stared up at me from the floor. I stood over him, panting hard.

'Get out!' he snarled, but I didn't need to be persuaded.

Without another word, furious, frustrated and in despair, I turned for the door and slammed it shut behind me.

'I'm gone,' I said to myself, and like a balm the breeze blowing across from the Lakes cooled my face.

6

New Horizons

I COULD BARELY AFFORD THE RENT on my first home. It took up most of my pay packet, but that didn't matter: I was free from my stepfather at last. The place I'd found was just outside Penrith, slightly exposed to the elements, perhaps, and yet still somewhere I could call my own. Basically, a cramped little cottage, it was badly in need of decoration and with a nosy neighbour who watched my every move. It also had an outside toilet.

At first, I found my new place quite funny. I was nice to the lady next door, even though she practically knew what I ate for breakfast, lunch and dinner. I also laughed about heading outside to use the loo. Then winter came. In Cumbria, it's the season for a unique, strong and relentless northeasterly to roll down off the mountains. The helm wind, as it's known, can be testing at the best of times, but not fun at all when it's also driving in snow and you can't get into the toilet because of the drift against the door.

It was in the grip of one bitterly cold spell that I began to think about my dad. He had been gone for some time, but we remained in touch. Once in a blue moon I would receive a letter or a phone call. Things were great on the other side of the world, so he said. The sun was always shining and his career back on track. The move had been the making of him, he told me, and if I wished to join him then it could prove to be the opportunity of a lifetime.

Having cut all ties with my stepfather, I decided that it was time to take up his offer. I'd saved enough money from working all hours at the bakery and was beginning to feel burned out by the job. As I saw things, this was the perfect opportunity.

Mum didn't want me to go, of course. She kept flagging up that he couldn't be trusted, but in his absence, I had come to idolise him.

'He's my dad,' was all I had to say in reasoning with her and eventually she stopped objecting.

Shortly before Christmas that year, I booked a return flight to Queensland, Australia. In my heart, however, I hoped that it would be a one-way trip. I would move in with my dad, work alongside him and then support him through his later years. As for all the turmoil we had been through, as the plane touched down, I considered that to be in the past.

'At last! It's so good to see you!'

My dad was waiting for me when I walked out of Arrivals. He looked in good shape, with a tan that reflected his new life. He was cheerful, conversational and kept repeating on the drive back that this would be the start of something amazing for us both.

Within a matter of days, I realised I had made a huge mistake.

I had half-expected a cool reception from my stepmother. We had never really bonded, after all, but the first real alarm bell rang that evening when Dad offered me a drink. I accepted, and then watched him consume his hungrily. I went to bed that night hoping it was a one-off. A moment of celebration to mark being reunited with his son. Then Dad went to work the next morning, late and with a hangover, and reached for the bottle as soon as he got home. In the run-up to this trip, chatting to him over the phone, I had often noted that he sounded animated or slurred his words. Even so, it was as if I had a filter in my head that tuned out the things I didn't want to hear. Face to face, I couldn't ignore it.

My father was still in the teeth of alcoholism, and continued to project himself as if everything was just fine. On those days when he took me out sightseeing, he'd always be anxious about returning home by four o'clock. Then, he'd work his way through up to eight bottles of beer as an appetiser for the bottle of gin that followed. I would look at my stepmother in horror, but she seemed complicit to me: it was as if perhaps this was a way of keeping him under control.

A few days passed for my dad before the novelty of my presence back in his life wore off. That's when he stopped treating me as an adult and returned to menacing me as he had when I was growing up. With his short temper and intoxicated state of mind, I quickly fell back into the pattern of avoiding him where possible. Instead of tying up loose ends for me, and shedding some light on the circumstances for the divorce, he just returned to scoring points against my mum and fishing for details of her life without him.

It was a heartbreaking and demoralising experience. Rather than looking forward to a new start, I began to wish I had never made the trip at all. I became acutely homesick, in fact, to the point where I even missed the merciless helm wind and the sight of my neighbour shrinking from her window whenever I glanced at her house.

When Christmas came, a time for family, I felt completely excluded. Queensland is a beautiful part of the world, and I could see why my father had settled there, but it was a far cry from Cumbria. Every time I made the effort, Dad was just out of it, while the temperature dropped whenever I tried to talk to my stepmother. Things came to a head on New Year's Eve. Dad had insisted that I come to a big party with them, even though my stepmother seemed less than keen on the idea. Over the course of my stay, I had met one or two of their friends, who had been very nice to me, and so I felt it would be better than staying at home and stewing. As it turned out, I quite enjoyed myself. Everyone was in high spirits, of course, which proved a nice distraction. Then, as the clock ticked towards midnight, everything changed.

I had been sitting at a big table with my father, stepmother and their friends. Dad had risen unsteadily to his feet and declared that he was going to the bar. He took orders from everyone and left me facing my stepmother across the chair he'd just vacated. Amid the chatter and laughter, in that dimly lit function room swirling with cigarette smoke, she fixed her gaze upon me. Then she shared what had clearly been on her mind since my arrival.

'Whatever your father's promised you,' she said in a calm, purposeful voice, 'there's nothing for you here.'

Completely taken aback, I simply stared back at her for a moment.

'Is that why you think I've come all this way?' I asked, blinking finally. 'For some kind of ... *inheritance*?'

My stepmother said nothing in response. She just sat back, folded her arms and tightened her lips.

'Go home, Kerry,' she said finally, just as the countdown to midnight began.

I glanced at my father at the bar. He was negotiating his way back through the throng with the drinks for our table. He looked so unsteady I wasn't sure he'd make it this far. I rose to my feet, but not to help him.

'You're welcome to it all,' I said before turning my back on them all.

It was to be the last words I ever shared with my stepmother.

That night, I stayed with some friends I had made during my stay. My dad came round the next morning. By all accounts, my departure had caused quite a drama. Despite the fresh light of day, however, my mind was made up. Nothing had changed, I told him. Above all, I couldn't deal with his drinking.

'I'll stop,' he promised me, spreading his hands apart. 'From now on, I'll stick to orange juice.'

I had heard it all before and I think he knew it. Eventually, he just gave up in frustration, leaving me to ask my friends if they would drop me at the airport. All my stuff was at my dad's house, but I had no intention of going back there. Not only had we driven for hours across Queensland to attend this party, all I wanted to do was fly home. I was dressed in board shorts, a shirt and sandals. I had my passport and wallet. Following a phone call to book a last-minute flight, and with the airport just a short hop from where I was staying, I asked my friends to drive me directly there.

I made the departure gate with minutes to spare and ran up the stairs to board the plane. There would be no going back. I just clipped on my seatbelt, shut my eyes as we lifted into the air, and knew that I would never return. I had ventured out with high hopes and left feeling more alone than ever before. My father was a complete stranger. His love for the bottle overshadowed everything. At the same time, I wasn't prepared to let this episode drag me down. I was determined something positive should come from it. If I wanted to get on in life, I resolved on that long flight, then it was down to me to make that happen.

Back in Cumbria, I sent my dad a letter. I set out my reasons for coming back and finished with the line: 'We are two different people, and I'm so sorry you'll never know the real me.' If that was intended to draw a line across our relationship, the phone call I received from him by return just sealed it. He was blotto, stumbling in and out of words as he assured me everything would be just fine. Calmly and politely, I stopped him mid-sentence and told him that I had to go.

Following my return from Australia, I made several big decisions in a short space of time. First, I gave up drinking. I had seen what it did to my dad and didn't want to follow in his footsteps in any shape or form. Next, I took up a driving job with an agricultural merchant. As well as being a nine-to-five job, behind the wheel once more, I learned there was an element of salesmanship involved. Having enjoyed my time dealing with customers from behind the counter at the butcher's, this job offered me the best of both worlds. I soon found myself taking a truck loaded with products to build working relationships with farmers across the Lake District. It was hard work, but left me fit as a fiddle. It was also really good fun and did wonders for my confidence.

With the change of job came an opportunity to move on from the cottage. By now, I had grown tired of the outside toilet and the surveillance from my neighbour. I heard on the grapevine that a flat was becoming available for rent at a grand lodge house northeast of Penrith in Glassonby. It was owned by a local landowner called Robin and his family. I recognised the name from my dealings with local farmers. The lodge, when I visited to find out if the let was still available, enclosed a large courtyard. The flat itself was situated above the entrance to the courtyard. Even before I had knocked on the door, I knew I wanted to live here. It was set far back from the road with impressive grounds and sweeping views of the countryside.

'Would 12 pounds a week be acceptable?' Robin's wife asked me, after we had chatted and it turned out her husband was a customer at the agricultural supplier where I worked. I told her that was fine, and then she asked if I might be prepared to help out her husband around the grounds for a reduction in rent. 'I can pay you three pounds an hour to cut the grass,' she said, having taken me around to the sheds to show me the equipment I'd need to use.

I took one look at the ride-on mower and knew this was the place I wanted to be.

It was the easiest and most enjoyable chore I have ever done. The grounds were big enough for me to pay off my rent by riding around on the mower one afternoon a week. Not only that, I found life at the lodge suited me just fine: I liked the space, peace and quiet. Within a short space of time it truly felt like home.

It was Robin who took me under his wing. With his winter-white hair and weather-beaten features, this was a man who appeared to have spent his life outdoors. On that basis alone, I warmed to him immediately. A natural-born countryman, he was as kind and generous with his time as he was passionate about forestry land management. With me, his new lodger, he found a willing student. I would join Robin on walks and help him to bed in saplings and clear out undergrowth. He taught me which trees grew well against another and would set about planting new woodland so that future generations could enjoy it. The more I learned, the greater the responsibilities he gave to me, from catching eels to clearing magpies from hedgerows before they stole the eggs from other birds' nests, until I spent almost all my free time working alongside him. Together, we planted countless saplings across his estates. It wasn't a job, he didn't strong-arm me into it, it just came down to a shared love of the outdoors and the countryside, while his wife, Anne, and adult children came to treat me as one of their own.

This was the family I had never had. I like to think they adopted me, but in truth, I adopted them. Robin was an exemplary man and I came to consider him as a father figure. I had my flat, and my independence, but more often than not, he would call up to say that they were having fish and chips and invite me to eat with them. Along with my job selling to farmers, it provided me with a solid foundation at last. My happiness grew along with my love of the countryside. It also allowed me to give something back, which is how Zak came into my life.

7

About Zak

ROBIN KEPT LABRADORS AS GUNDOGS. Managing his land responsibly, which involved maintaining healthy stocks of grouse and pheasant, he trained his dogs to work for him on the shoots he hosted. Following the last crackle of rifle fire, I would watch him instruct them to head into the heather and scrub. Minutes later, they would return to his side, feathered prizes clasped gently in their jaws.

As their master, Robin was always consistent with his dogs. He kept them engaged and they adored him. Wherever he went, his dogs accompanied him. They needed him, and I wanted to feel like a dog needed me. I liked the Labs, but sometimes people would show up for the shoot with Springer Spaniels to work alongside them. Come lunchtime, when the Labs would often be flagging, it was the Springers who watched everyone drift back towards the lodge with an expression that said, 'Why are we stopping?' Their energy was boundless, and I admired them for it. Also, I hadn't forgotten the bond I'd shared with Prince, our Springer Cocker cross, whenever things got rough at home. Having enjoyed time with half a

Springer Spaniel, I decided now was the time to go all the way.

I bought Zak as a 12-week-old puppy from a place near Appleby. Springers are similar in appearance to their Cocker counterparts, but they're longer and more muscular. I didn't really know what I'd let myself in for as Zak grew bigger and more boisterous, but he became a good friend. I wanted him to become a gun dog so he could work with me across the estates, so I took him to a gun dog trainer, but the experience wasn't great for Zak or me. The trainer took us into a field. There, he asked me to make my dog sit.

'Sit,' I said, and Zak responded by heading for the hills.

'Do it again,' said the trainer when Zak came back, 'but this time do it properly.'

I stood up straight and raised my hand.

'Sit!' I commanded, and repeated myself when Zak just looked baffled. '*Sit!*'

With a sigh, the trainer called him to heel.

'It's time to show who's the boss here,' he said.

Before I could ask if he was talking to me or Zak, the trainer reached for the poor dog and scooped him up against his chest. To my horror, he then threw Zak down onto the ground and pinned him there.

'Hey, that's my dog!' I protested when he finally let go, while Zak climbed to his feet a trembling mess and looked at me as if to say, 'Who is this guy?'

It wasn't an approach that worked for me. I recognised that dogs need to know who is boss, but felt this should be driven by respect, not dominance. So, I took Zak home and decided to train him myself. It was a hit-and-miss affair, a case of winging it and trying to understand Zak. I had Robin to call upon, of course, and he provided sound advice based on his experience with dogs.

Once Zak and I had mastered the basics, I decided to have a go at gun dog training myself. Robin grew tomatoes in his garden. Using the ripest I could find that were nicely soft and squishy, I placed three on the ground behind the dog. Then, using hand gestures, I indicated to Zak which tomato I wanted him to fetch for me. Zak had to learn which way to turn, and then be gentle to avoid puncturing the tomatoes. Finally, after a lot of hard work, everything clicked. All of a sudden, I had a dog that retrieved, and we quickly moved on to picking up feathers so that he could get used to the tickly feeling between his jaws and not instinctively spit them out. I was so proud of him and pleased that we followed our own path. If anything, it brought us closer together.

The result? I had a fully trained Springer Spaniel who was also massively hyperactive. They all are, it's in their bones. As a young dog, Zak was permanently full of beans. I found that he was most responsive to my command once I'd taken the edge off his energy. So, ahead of a shoot, with people paying thousands of pounds to take part and not wishing to be bothered by a mad Spaniel, I'd take him for a ride in the Land Rover. With the dog wailing with excitement, I'd head for a big field, drop him off and then just drive around the perimeter several times. Zak would bound alongside the vehicle, full of enthusiasm, but to be honest, it never really wore him out. If anything, he just got fitter.

Having left my childhood behind, I grew to love my life
with the Rowleys. Zak was at the heart of it. I could spend
a day up on the moors in the howling wind and rain, then
return to my flat for supper with a wet dog steaming in
front of the log fire for company. I adored Zak and the
feeling was mutual. He went everywhere with me outside
of work hours and stayed with Robin and his family whenever I set out in the van. From time to time, he even came
with me and that just made me so happy.

After several years in the post I could sell almost anything
to my customer base, from animal feed to hardware and
heavy-duty clothing. I strove to strike deals to exceed my
targets and became increasingly driven. Eventually, my
hard work came to the attention of a rival agricultural
supplier. They offered me a job package that in theory I
couldn't refuse, with better money and a company car. The
catch, I discovered, came down to the fact that if I wanted
to do the job effectively then I would have to move closer
to the business in West Cumbria.

I adored my life with the Rowleys and I didn't want to
move. At the same time, I had become quite career-minded.
All the hard work I had put into the estate had helped me
to shine and I suppose I wanted to prove to myself that I
was no longer the frightened little boy who did his level
best to avoid attention from those who were supposed to
be watching out for him. So, I took the job, with the promise of a company car and a pay hike, and within weeks of
moving, I started to wonder if I had made the right decision. Zak came with me, but it was a completely different
lifestyle. I bought my first home, a semi-detached in a town

called Dearham. It was nice, but felt like a world away from where I felt comfortable. Despite a handsome coast-line nearby, I felt adrift and a little cooped up in a house that came to remind me of my father's old place under the railway bridge. To make things harder, I couldn't bring Zak to work with me. Instead, I had to rely on the kindness of neighbours to mind him each day.

I worked hard to make a success of the job, because frankly, I didn't want to admit to myself that I had given up on an existence that meant so much to me. Whenever possible, we would go back and stay with the Rowleys. Zak always turned circles with excitement when he saw Robin and his family and it was great to spend time with my friend and mentor. Whenever we went walking, we would pass through growing woodland we had planted years before. There's something so special about that, which just made me miss my old life on the fells even more.

Sometimes I would stay the weekend and go out with friends on a Saturday night. One time, we headed into nearby Keswick for a drink. The centre was always humming with life. On that particular evening, a pretty young woman with a cheeky smile called Angela caught my eye. A hairdresser who worked from a salon in her home, she liked to chat and laugh. Basically, she was a people person. To my surprise she seemed interested in my life. Shyness got the better of me, but Angela had a sparkle I could only admire. We had a few drinks and arranged to meet the next weekend. I liked her a lot. In fact, I had the weirdest sense that one day I would marry her. Even before

I drove back to Dearham for another week's work, I had begun to look forward to that first date.

Then Zak got ill, out of nowhere, and I couldn't see beyond the next day.

8

Loss and Love

IT BEGAN WITH A SKIPPED MEAL. I gave Zak his breakfast and he just showed no interest. When he refused his supper, I called the vet and took the earliest appointment. Following a check-up, they decided to monitor him for a week. Zak barely ate in that time. We returned for a scan and when the vet reported back on the findings, he suggested a small exploratory operation.

'It's just a precaution,' he said, 'so we can be sure there's nothing to worry about.'

I dropped Zak off with the vet before work. I didn't make a huge fuss of him because I wanted him to be relaxed when I left. Besides, I planned to finish early and pick him up so he'd be nicely settled for the evening. So, when my phone rang towards lunchtime I began to think about clocking off before I'd even picked up.

'Mr Irving?' I recognised the vet's voice immediately. I also wondered why he would be making such a routine call instead of the nurse. He cleared his throat. 'Kerry, I need you to know that if there's anything we could have done to save Zak, we would have done so without hesitation.'

'*What?*'

It felt like I was a heartbeat behind everything the vet went on to tell me. He explained that on opening up Zak, they found he was suffering from late-stage cancer. It was everywhere, he said, and inoperable. Realistically, he assured me, the kindest thing they could do was to let him go.

I understood, I really did, yet the news destroyed me. Zak had been a part of my life for nine years. It was like being told I'd just lost my best mate. Not only that, I felt as if I'd missed out on my chance to say goodbye to him. That was one of the most challenging parts of the whole grieving process, which hit me hard. At the same time, years of burying my feelings away meant I did exactly the same thing over Zak. I went back to work, a little more subdued than usual, but nobody knew that on the inside I was broken. At the end of each day I'd go home and the house would feel like an empty shell. I found it suffocating being there. Zak's presence was everywhere, and yet he was gone.

In the weeks after his death, I decided I could never replace Zak. We had formed a bond and it was only on losing him that I had come to realise how much he meant to me. Dogs, I decided, were no longer for me – I just couldn't handle the heartbreak.

Although I could bury my feelings, I felt I needed to tell Angela when I saw her. She seemed like someone I could talk to, but I didn't let it dominate our date or the one after that. Angela came from a family that had never kept pets. No dog had ever set a paw inside their house, in fact. So, whenever we were together, I just focused on enjoying our time together rather than dwelling on the past. Over time, as our relationship deepened, it helped me to move on. Angela knew how much Zak had meant to me, but by then we had fallen in love and were planning our future together. I never forgot Zak, and the bond we formed, but in many ways Angela arrived in my life at exactly the right time. She didn't retrieve the same as a Spaniel, but smelled better, and ultimately, we made each other happy.

In 1998, Angela and I got married. I also took up a new job, which allowed me to sell my house and relocate back across the Lakes to join my new wife in Keswick. A market town in the heart of the fells, with views to the southwest across Derwentwater Lake to the forested slopes beyond, it seemed like a world of its own. Angela had lived there all her life, and within no time at all, it felt like my home too. With such extremes in elevation from the water's edge to the mountain summits, we could have all kinds of weather in one day. From one hour to the next, great storm clouds could roll in and then break apart to let sunshine stream through. When it rained, it fell in drifts, sailing down on winds shaped and funnelled by our surroundings. Through my eyes, blissfully newlywed, there was nowhere else like it, no other place I wanted to be.

Without Zak, who loved nothing more than a countryside walk, I found myself looking for reasons to go out. I still enjoyed being outdoors, but often Angela would be busy with her work and it wasn't the same on my own. I had a mate who enjoyed mountain biking. It looked like a good way to enjoy my surroundings and so I invested in one. With forests and fell paths just a short ride from our house, I quickly fell in love with cycling. It was also a good way to meet people, I discovered. Within a short space of time, I had a new circle of friends with a shared interest. It also proved to be a good stress reliever from work as I continued to climb the career ladder in agricultural sales.

For a lad who had struggled with self-confidence, my drive was now second to none. I moved from one firm to another, slowly ascending in position and responsibility, and with ever increasing budgets. In pursuit of a good deal, I even began to develop quite a ruthless streak. But it didn't come naturally to me, it was just something required in order for me to do my job to the best of my abilities. At the end of each day, I'd come home feeling frazzled to an empty house. Rather than wait around for Angela, I'd immediately jump on my bike. I was one of those 'work hard, play hard' kind of people. Frankly, I thrived on the pressure and the release from it. Even if my wife happened to be at home when I got back, I would yearn to just hit the road.

'How about a walk around the lake?' she would sometimes suggest.

'Lovely,' I'd say and force a smile. 'Shall I go for a ride before or after?'

'Oh, let's just go now,' she'd say, and I'd find myself whisking her round in a bid to get back so I could climb into the saddle and chill out.

As the years ticked by, and my responsibilities grew, I found myself in charge of sales on a national level. I was also increasingly deskbound, running a department for a company in Lancaster. That meant commuting by car from Keswick for an hour each way every day. It was exhausting but that didn't take the edge off my desire to ride out onto the trails whenever I had the opportunity. It might have been sparked by the loss of a faithful friend, but I found mountain biking to be fulfilling in different ways. I'd come home splattered in mud but with a grin on my face. Angela would order me to shower and then afterwards I'd join her, feeling clean, tired and content. It was a good life, even when my interest extended from mountain biking to road cycling. I found that rather than doing 15 miles over a mountain in one hour, I could do 40, 50 or even 60 miles in one session. The only hitch was that session could last the best part of a day, which took care of my weekends.

Come Saturday, Angela would drop me off in Penrith before heading to the shops and I would cycle home. Only I'd do so via Cumbria's west coast, coming back across the Lakes. I'd return home buzzing, because frankly, it was an addiction. I was constantly reviewing my performance, looking at ways to improve, and that reflected my outlook on work. During one particular sales push, my boss at the time took me to one side and suggested it was okay to fail sometimes. I just didn't get it.

'Why?' I asked. 'Who wants to fail?'

I had spent my entire childhood believing I wasn't good enough to feel wanted or loved. Now I had it all, from a loving wife to a challenging job and an all-consuming outdoor pursuit. I had everything, and wanted to make the most of it. Focused on the road ahead, I was determined to live my life to the fullest, with no sense that something could close in from behind and threaten to take it all away.

Back at the tent, looking up at the summit of Ben Nevis in the late afternoon light, I feel euphoric. I am exhausted, tested beyond my limits, but together with Max, I had conquered that mountain.

Beside me, flat on his side and with a stick in his mouth, Max meets my eye as if to say, 'What a great day!'

'It's been the best,' I reply out loud, as I often do as part of our imaginary conversation. He looks so happy and content, which is exactly how I feel. 'Yeah, we've done this.'

With all the planning and preparation and doubts about whether I could pull it off, I realise that I hadn't thought beyond getting to the top of the mountain. All my focus and attention had been on how I would make the climb. Now that it's behind us, however, I find I can't face the long and punishing road journey home – it would just be too much stress on my back. We are both exhausted, and my spine is needling me, but above all, I don't want this moment to end. So, after a good night's sleep in the tent, with Max curled up beside me, I decide we should head west across Scotland. With my Spaniel riding shotgun, we take the scenic route over several hours to the coast south of Mallaig.

I had heard the coastline there is impressive, with silver-white sands and views across to the Small Isles of Rum, Eigg, Muck and Canna. Sure enough, having found a campsite right opposite a long beach, I find the sight exceeds my expectations. What's more, as I set off for a long, laboured walk along the shoreline, under Max's close eye, it feels like we're the only two living beings on earth. The water is a deep blue, sparkling under sunshine. The islands on the horizon could harbour buried treasure while the surf underfoot has delivered a tideline of sea-worn treasures for Max. Almost immediately, he finds a piece of driftwood and takes it with him on his investigation of the rock pools. I can only dream of padding along so effortlessly. I'm still in so much pain from the climb, but now it seems like something that cannot defeat me. I'm not frightened of it any more, it doesn't own me. Instead, carrying my shoes and with my trousers rolled above my ankles, I float along the water's edge and feel transported.

In my mind, I am back in South Africa; a little boy once more with not a care in the world and no sense of the horrors that awaited me on our return to the UK. At the same time, I recognise that those formative years are behind me now. I had survived a challenging childhood and found myself as a young man, thanks to a countryman who shared my love of the outdoors, and dear Zak. Now, in my forties, I can look back on all the events that have shaped my life since then and say to myself that I am one lucky chap. I had been through hell, both unforeseen and life-changing, and yet with support from my wife, I have come through it with the best friend anyone could ask for: Max. My saviour, my protector, my inspiration and my guiding light.

Part Two

9

The Accident

THE SUMMER OF 2006 WAS LONG and hot across the Lake District. The grass and heather faded in colour as the ground dried out and the only cool breeze to be found was at the very summit of the fells. It wasn't the kind of weather to be cooped up inside a car, travelling to and from work.

My department was preparing for a big event at an agricultural trade show. The team were putting in extra hours to make sure that our stand would be up and running, and I was doing everything I could to support them. We had put in an order at a printer in Kendal for promotional material. When the call came through to confirm that it was ready for collection, I volunteered to drive across and pick it up on my way home. It wasn't too far out of the way, and I could at least check we had everything we needed.

Rush hour in the northwest of England is the same as it is anywhere in the world. Even in a rural area such as this, the volume of traffic simply means that at some point in the journey, everyone is going to crawl. Approaching Keswick, with a box of glossy brochures in a box in the back, I slowed behind a small queue of cars waiting to pull out at a busy junction. I was driving a company Audi Estate with the kind of air conditioning that could take all the discomfort out of a hot day. After Angela and my bikes, I considered the car to be my pride and joy. I washed it on a regular basis, and lived in fear of ever finding a scratch or a dent on it. With the car at the head of the queue showing no sign of moving, I pulled up the handbrake and let the cooled air from the dashboard fan wash over me. I peeled forward from my seat, keen to let the air reach my back, which was sticky in my work shirt. I kept my eyes on the tail lights of the car in front, waiting for some sign of movement. When it came, however, my attention turned automatically to the rear-view mirror. There, to the sound of squealing brakes, I saw the grill of a fast-approaching truck fill my field of vision.

The impact that followed was so loud it seemed like a bomb had just detonated inside my car. I slammed back against the headrest before jerking forwards. My seat belt restrained me but the shunt was intense and caused the air bag to go off. I remember gasping for breath, in shock at what had just happened, and then slumped back in a sudden, eerie stillness.

My car had been slammed from behind by a lorry. The driver had misjudged his braking and shunted into me. Reeling, I climbed out, into the heat of the day. I had missed the car in front by an inch, but the back of my vehicle had simply crumpled.

'Are you okay?'

By now, people had rushed from their cars to check on me. I don't recall exactly how I responded. A surge of adrenalin masked any sense of shock and at the time it appeared that I had escaped serious injury. My neck was sore, but that was no surprise given the force of the impact.

'I'll survive,' I said, and focused my attention on getting my Audi moved to the side of the road so that I could exchange details with the lorry driver.

By the time I parked outside my house, in a car that would need some serious repair work done to the body at the back, the reality of my situation had begun to kick in. The Audi, I realised, was the least of my concerns. In many ways, it had done its job and absorbed much of the force from being struck by the truck. That could've killed me, I acknowledged to myself, as Angela hurried out of the house. I had called to let her know that I'd been involved in an accident and she mustn't worry about me. In the time it took for me to drive back to Keswick, she had called her dad. He was a retired ambulance man and a no-nonsense kind of guy.

'I'm taking you to the hospital,' he insisted at my door, 10 minutes later. 'You need to get checked over.'

'I'll be fine,' I insisted. 'I don't feel great, but I'm sure it'll pass.'

My father-in-law stepped aside and drew my attention to his Fiat Panda.

'Get in,' he ordered.

I didn't feel I had much to report to the triage doctor who saw me. I'd been hit by a truck from behind. Now, my back and my head were beginning to ache. In my view, I just needed a good night's sleep. Having checked me over, he advised me to make an appointment with my doctor the next day just to be on the safe side.

I glanced at my father-in-law. His expression told me I would have to do just that.

The following morning, I woke to find that I wasn't any better. I felt dizzy and sick, like I had climbed off a roller coaster, while my upper back was increasingly uncomfortable. My main concern at the time, however, was work. With the trade show looming this was not a good moment to be off, but by the time I had made it downstairs it was clear to me that I'd need to call in sick. I felt like I was abandoning my department, but was so unwell that I didn't think I'd be any use.

'Adrenalin is a natural painkiller,' my doctor said after having examined me. 'It would've flooded through your system in response to the crash, but now that's wearing off, so if you're feeling bad now then you're going to feel terrible over the next week or so.'

She had asked me to describe the crash, wincing as I recounted how I had seen the lorry in my rear-view mirror in the moment before impact. Her view was that a vehicle of that size hitting my stationary car would have led to a big transfer of energy, much of which was likely to have travelled through my spine. The fact that I couldn't come close to touching my toes without experiencing jarring pain seemed to bear this out.

'What kind of recovery time am I looking at?' I asked, mindful of work.

'You need to be patient,' my doctor told me.

'Are we talking days?'

'Kerry, I would suggest resting for a couple of weeks,' she said, which took me by surprise, and set about writing out a prescription for painkillers. 'Just be ready to take these on a regular basis.'

I've always been the sort of person who places great faith in medical professionals, so, armed with my prescription and keen to get back on my feet, I did exactly as I was told. Feeling dizzy, sick and with my back increasingly in spasms, I extended my sick leave from work and effectively sat at home for a fortnight. I tried to sleep it off, but every time I closed my eyes, I just relived the accident. With Angela at work, cutting hair in her salon upstairs, I spent most of my time in front of daytime television. Customers would come and go, sounding cheery in the hallway as my wife saw them in and out, which only made me feel even more cut off from the outside world in the living room next door.

It was tough, having gone from living my life at full tilt to just slumping in front of the screen with the curtains shut against the midday sun. I started stewing about it, because with every day that passed, I felt no better. I'd also made plans with a friend to cycle from coast to coast and that went on hold indefinitely. At the same time, whenever I moved, I found my back caused me problems. I'd get shooting pains down my arms and legs that were so bad on occasion that I'd cry out. Even when I did find a way onto my feet it was little more than a careful shuffle. Alongside this, I found my headaches mounted until they became completely blinding.

'I feel no better,' I told the doctor at the next check-up. 'If anything, it's getting worse.'

I found it hard to communicate just what kind of pain I was in. Part of my problem was that everything I was complaining about had worsened since the accident. I had walked away from it, thinking I would be fine after a cup of tea, and now a trip to my local GP surgery left me absolutely flattened. My doctor checked me over and decided to increase my painkiller dosage. Frankly, that did nothing to help. After a few weeks I made an attempt to return to work. I felt lousy for leaving my department to handle the trade show without me. All I wanted was to get behind my desk, but when I finally made it to the office I was in agony.

It wasn't long before I had to see my doctor again to sign off sick on a long-term basis. I was embarrassed about my repeat visits. Before the accident, I wasn't even sure I'd know how to find my local surgery. Now, I was a regular in the waiting room. Despite understanding and sympathy from every GP I saw, I would still find myself sent away with yet more medication.

With summer long gone, I had left behind the fit, outgoing man that everyone knew me to be. Instead, I had become a shell of my former self. With every day, week and month that passed, I experienced no end to the pain. I lived in hope for quite a while, expecting to wake up one morning and find at least some improvement. If anything, it felt like I was steadily seizing up and any attempt to break free could leave me writhing in agony.

As winter approached, I found it difficult to function normally. Even dressing had become a struggle. I couldn't lift my arms without a terrible burning sensation in the back of my neck. Almost every move I made caused my bones to crunch. Alongside this, the drugs turned my brain to mush. I'd started on codeine and then progressed to tramadol and then the kind of morphine products that leave you unsure if it's half past four in the afternoon or a poached egg. I existed in a fog of confusion, with a fuse on my patience that became shorter as time ticked by.

Throughout this time, poor Angela had to watch her husband sliding into helplessness. A trooper by nature, she did everything in her power to support me. She worked longer hours, taking on more customers in a bid to cover some of the income I had dropped, and effectively ran the household. Whenever I returned from the doctor, downcast because there seemed to be no plan for my recovery, she insisted I return and push for further tests. Angela encouraged me to try out physio and even alternative therapies. That helped to relax me, but the constant pain I experienced was exhausting. By the turn of the year, I was existing in limbo, broken in so many ways, and my mood began to darken.

Before the accident, and in the years following Zak's passing, cycling had become central to my life. It helped me to deal with stress at work and kept me connected to the outside world. With no hope of climbing onto a bike, I missed this aspect of my life terribly. I longed to join my friends on the road, but eventually gave up, promising I would soon be back. To begin with, they visited and bantered and wished me well, but as time progressed, those knocks at the door became few and far between. I suppose

I just wasn't much fun to be around, but it left me feeling even more isolated and resentful that this had happened to me. I would moan to Angela that we had always been perfect hosts after a big ride out. My cycling buddies would cram into the kitchen for tea and cake, but now here I was crying out for company and they had basically abandoned me. That's how I viewed things, as if fate had taken my life and scrunched it up like a ball of wastepaper.

With no glimmer of improvement with every day that passed, living with chronic pain and a medication regime that messed with my mind, I soon found myself sliding into a pit of despair.

10

A Cold, Dark Place

'ANGELA? Angela, help me!'

I was lying in a heap on the bathroom tiles. I couldn't move. Not without risk of being struck by another bolt of crippling pain that had just dropped me to the floor when I stepped out of the shower. Over time, I had learned not to lift my arms too high. That was a trigger, but sometimes the slightest movement of a muscle could leave me feeling like my spinal cord had just become electrified, as it had now.

'What's happened? Kerry!'

Angela had rushed from the kitchen on hearing me cry out and hit the ground with a thud. This wasn't the first time it had occurred. I could be making a cup of tea, brushing my teeth or just turning my head when the phone rang. Anything as slight as this could push the button in my neck that shut my body down in agony. Just then, as she tried to ease me into a robe, I began to sweat with the pain. No matter how gently she attempted to manoeuvre me, I would catch my breath and grimace as if the muscles in my body were in the grip of invisible vices.

'I can't take much more of this,' I said as she struggled to raise me to my feet. I'm a broad-shouldered fellow and my wife is only little. Even so, poor Angela supported me every step of the way on the long, painful journey down the stairs to the car.

We had made this kind of emergency trip to the hospital on numerous occasions since the accident. This time, we found ourselves waiting for four hours in A&E. When I did see a doctor, he prescribed yet more painkillers. Physically, the medication put me in a place where I could get through each day. Mentally, the damage slowly mounted. I felt like my head was stuffed with cloth. I couldn't process my thoughts and feelings properly, and slowly my world around me shrank. The countryside that had been so central to my life was no longer available to me. I could shuffle out to the post box, but didn't like doing it. If I had to go somewhere then I tended to just drive and even then, I'd find every excuse to stay at home – it felt like doors were closing on me from all directions.

Almost a year after the accident, I got my first appointment for an MRI scan. By then, I'd left my job as it was just too painful for me to travel to work. Having used up my savings, I was forced onto benefits, which did nothing for my self-esteem. It also meant I had to dig into my weekly budget to pay for the journey to a hospital on the other side of the county. I just hoped that something could be done. In a way, I was delighted when the scan showed I had suffered some damage to a spinal disc in my neck. In my mind, it proved I wasn't just making this up. Until then, the cause of all the pain I was in had proved a mystery. Now, everyone could see that it was originating from damage to my nerves sustained in the accident and understood why I experienced it at such devastating intensity.

'So, you can treat it now?' I asked the consultant who took me through the scan report.

In response, furrowing his brow, he told me the answer could only come with more tests.

In the weeks that followed the results, I was sent from one back specialist to another, each of whom gave me a differing opinion. One said he could resolve things with a simple operation, another cautioned that any kind of procedure could cripple me, while everyone else had an opinion somewhere between the two. It was as frustrating as it was confusing and left me with the view that, somehow, I needed to find a way around the pain. I had come to live with the threat of dropping to the floor in agony with one false move, but didn't want to risk ending up in a wheelchair just to be free from it. Somehow, I had to find a way to own the pain. I just didn't know how, and on the final consultation that fact left me close to tears.

'There must be something,' I asked, wiping my eyes with the heel of my hand. 'Anything!'

The invitation, when it came, sounded less risky than an operation, but better than doing nothing. It wasn't a cure, the consultant cautioned, but if everything went well then it would take the edge off the pain for a while so I could get on with rebuilding my life. A cervical epidural, as the procedure was called, involved a steroid injection into the lower part of the neck to reduce the inflammation and calm the nerves. I agreed to it before he'd even finished outlining what I could expect.

'It's just a needle,' I told Angela in unusually high spirits when I returned home. 'After all this time, an injection could be the answer to my problems.'

I showed up for my appointment assuming I would be in and out in no time. Having filled out a form, I was asked to sit in a busy waiting room for admission to the day ward. It wasn't quite what I expected, but I didn't complain. Every now and then, the ward sister would show up and call out a name from a list. One by one, every man and woman left the waiting room until I was the only one left. I looked up hopefully when the ward sister returned and consulted her clipboard.

'Kerry Irving?' she said, ignoring me and straining to see if anyone was around the corner at the hot drinks machine. 'Kerry?'

'That's me,' I said, which earned her full attention.

'Oh.' She seemed to take a moment to regroup her thoughts. 'I'm sorry, I saw the name Kerry and just assumed ...'

'I was a woman,' I said, and broke into a grin. 'You wouldn't be the first.'

Cheeks flushing, the ward sister ran the back of a biro down her list.

'I'm afraid we have no more beds in the men's ward,' she said. 'They've all been allocated and, well, we can't find you a bed with the women.' The staff nurse paused, looked up at me and then shrugged. 'We'll have to put you in one of the private rooms,' she said. 'With a television.'

'The perks of having a girl's name,' I said and carefully rose from the chair to follow her.

By the time I was summoned for the procedure, ready and waiting in my hospital gown, I felt unusually relaxed. My back was less of a problem propped up on a bed, and with my own space, I'd managed to nap for a bit. Above all, I was looking forward to my first real taste of a dampening in the pain.

I had assumed I would hobble my way to a side room; I hadn't expected a hospital porter to show up with a gurney.

'We're off to get your heart checked first,' he explained, 'just to be sure you're strong enough to take the injection.'

'Oh, I think I can handle it,' I said with great confidence, but clambered on all the same.

With the results of the ECG confirming that I was in good health for a jab, I found myself duly wheeled through the corridors. It was only when we passed the third one marked 'THEATRE' that I wondered what exactly was in store.

'It's not as bad as it looks,' said the head of the team awaiting me, dressed in a mask, gown and surgical cap. 'Strictly speaking, this isn't an operation.'

'I was beginning to wonder!' I said as the porter helped me off the gurney.

The guy in charge gestured towards the operating table.

'We just need you to lean over this, we'll be finished in no time.'

So, I did as I was told. At the same time, the guy turned to collect a large medical instrument from the table. It looked like a mastic gun, I thought, with some trepidation.

'It's a special syringe,' said one of the two nurses who had come to flank me just then. Gently but firmly, each took hold of me by the shoulders. Even though I was being completely compliant, it felt as though they were restraining me. 'Just relax and it'll be over in no time.'

'You might feel a thud,' said the main man, as what felt not so much like a needle but the muzzle of a rifle touched the space between my shoulder blades. 'Are you ready?'

I reminded myself why I was there and told him to begin.

Several hours later, having spent time in recovery from what felt like a donkey kicking me in the back, I left the hospital in a wheelchair. I had driven to the appointment, unaware that it was recommended that someone drive me home.

'Is your wife here?' asked the porter as I climbed out of the wheelchair.

'She's waiting in the car,' I lied, and having said goodbye, did my level best to cross the car park without passing out.

When I finally felt fit enough to drive, later that afternoon I arrived home feeling sore but in good spirits. For the first time since the accident, I could walk into the house without feeling like I might be seized by pain at any moment.

'It's worked,' I told Angela. 'I really think this is it!'

My mood continued to lift as I discovered just what a difference the injection had made. I could raise my hands above my head or bend down to fetch a plate from the cupboard and these little movements didn't defeat me. All

I could do was grin and laugh and begin to feel like my former self.

Sadly, it was to be a window of relief that didn't stay open for long. Within a short space of time, the pain crept back into my life and with that came the despair I had been so desperate to leave behind.

I would go on to endure another five cervical epidurals. I passed out on the second one when the needle hit a bone, though it brought me relief for a month. The rest failed to work completely. After that, I simply gave up. It was as if I had cracked open a door to a pain-free future, only for it to shut in my face and lock tight. If anything, the experience just dropped me deeper into a hole.

I didn't once consider the fact that I might be depressed. In a way, I was too locked into my thoughts to register it. Not only did I tend to sit indoors all day, I became reluctant to go out at all. As the months ticked by, I even became fearful of it. Just thinking about a walk to get some fresh air would panic me. What if my back seized and I couldn't get home? There was no way that I could risk it, and so I festered in that front room and tried to find a space in my head where the pain couldn't reach me.

I will always be grateful to Angela for not giving up on me. I had become unrecognisable from the man she married, yet not once did she reach the limits of her patience. She may be slight in build, with a lovely pleasant manner, but very little fazes her. Inside, she's tough, and she'll do anything to protect me. Whenever those waves of pain crashed over me, she was there for me in practical mode, but we didn't talk about how I was feeling. For one thing, I never opened up to her. Instead, I went into lock-down as I had done growing up and just internalised everything. It wasn't healthy, of course, and over time all the negative emotions that had crept into my life became the governing force. I was angry at myself and the world outside, easily upset and prone to bouts of long, dark silences. The damage to my nerves had also left me incredibly sensitive to changes in temperature. I liked to keep the house warm at all times and became obsessive about it. Angela knew this, but there was no way she could appreciate just how the slightest chill could affect me.

One evening, we were watching television in the living room. The gas fire was on, which didn't offer much in the way of heat. I was sitting on the sofa. It was most comfortable for my back, but I didn't really benefit from the glowing bars like the armchair that Angela always favoured. It was the end of a long day at work for her, while I had just spent my time silently resenting my lot in life.

'I'll just put the kettle on,' she said during a break in the programme we were watching. 'Would you like a brew?'

'Sure,' I grunted as she left her seat. 'Ange, can you shut the door?' I added as she headed into the hallway for the kitchen. 'Ange!'

Despite raising my voice, she didn't return. Angela had been gone for a matter of seconds, but with my battered nerves, the draught from the hallway felt like an Arctic blast. I shouted for her again and bellowed a second time in both panic and anger.

'What's wrong?' she asked on finally returning. 'It's not that cold.'

'Not cold?' I was shivering and hugging myself to stay warm, also fuming on the inside. 'Angela, you have no idea what I'm going through. I'm stuck here, day after day. I've lost my job, my friends and my bike is covered in dust. I'm in terrible pain and I've seen countless experts, but nobody can do anything about it and so I just sit here, rattling with pills and trying not to move too much. This is my world!' I gestured wildly at the four walls. 'This is it, and I'm miserable!'

'You mustn't give up hope, Kerry.' Angela closed the door and crossed to her chair. 'I don't like you speaking this way.'

'Why not?' I spat back, cutting off her attempt to calm me. 'What have I got going for me, eh? Why should I bother living when I'm this miserable and dragging you down with me? It's not fair to either of us, Angela. I can't carry on like this, it's unbearable!'

For a moment, in the silence that fell upon us, Angela looked at me as if I had just spoken from a place she had never imagined I could be. From the kitchen the sound of the kettle coming to boil finished with a click.

'I'll make us that tea,' she said, and then invited me to sit in her place by the fire. 'And I want you to take my chair from now on.'

11

Out of Milk

LIVING WITH CHRONIC PAIN is exhausting. From the moment you wake up, it dominates your day and even keeps you from sleep. I found there was very little I could do to escape it. Despite every effort, it just fixed itself to my thoughts as much as the bones in my body. In a way, the injections did little more than taunt me. When they worked, they gave me a brief reminder of what life could be like without living in fear of contorting in agony, only for that respite to fade. Sometimes it lasted for a few weeks. Other times that blissful sense that my ordeal was over would be gone within days. Those that failed completely, however, just dragged me into further despair.

I took pills to manage the pain. Sometimes they rubbed the hard edge off things, or simply knocked me out for hours on end. I just took them religiously because I felt I had no other option available to me. Over time, my medication schedule became more important to me than when I ate or slept. First thing, I'd start my prescription routine and hope the effects kicked in quickly. It never left me completely free from pain, and as the day progressed, I'd feel it returning in force. Then I would count down the hours until the next dosage. Sometimes I'd find myself in so much discomfort that I'd take it early, and that would bring forward the next round. Eventually, I reached the point where I was relying on more pills than I should have been taking, which left me feeling disconnected from reality. With my head messed up by all the medication, this also fuelled a sense of great anxiety. I worried what would happen if I ran out of pills, for example, or somehow lost access to them. It became such a concern that eventually I used that as a reason not to leave the house at all.

Pain relief became my comfort blanket, but also kept me prisoner inside my own home.

I was never aware that I had slipped into the grip of depression. It was such a slow, creeping process that I didn't notice the way my mood and outlook changed. By the time that dark veil had settled over my life, I just focused on functioning rather than processing my feelings. So, when Angela had unwittingly left me in the living room with a cold draught, my outburst was driven by just how desperate and helpless I had become. For a short while after that episode, however, I felt less angry about my life, as if putting my negative thoughts into words had helped to release pressure. In her own way, Angela had shown that her loyalty and support knew no bounds. I felt bad about yelling at her, of course, but also relieved that at the same time I had also opened up; it just wasn't something I built on. Instead, having vented at my poor wife, I fell back into brooding. I felt wretched in my head, and broken in my own body, while the financial strain was horrendous. From the moment I signed off sick, I had dropped a hard-earned salary. All my savings had gone on supporting us this far and now I relied on Angela and her salon upstairs to keep the roof over our heads and food on the table. I couldn't even help out around the house and that really destroyed me. From doing the dishes to changing a lightbulb, every time I tried to pull my weight, I'd end up writhing in agony. And as time marched on, feeling like I was nothing but a burden, I began to seriously consider a way out that would end it all.

In the winter of 2009, three years after the accident, the surface of the lake froze over. That season, stuck indoors, I felt the cold in the marrow of my bones; no amount of extra layers or heating would keep it at bay. Miserable, medicated, I had lost all hope that anything or anyone could help me. It was Angela who told me that she had gone for a walk around the shoreline and watched children skating stones across the frozen surface. We agreed the ice probably wouldn't be that thick beyond the shallows, and that's when I saw myself walking out to test it for myself. The vision only lasted for a moment, but it was so clear, I felt transported. There I was, striding with a purpose, beyond caring about any pain I was in and unconcerned about being outside. As I saw things, I would walk about 30 to 40 yards from the shore, the ice would give way under my feet with a splintering crack, and that would be it: I'd go under and the lake would claim me.

I should have been shocked at entertaining such a thought. Instead, it just triggered a series of impulsive urges to take my own life. Several times, while driving to and from hospital appointments that just got me nowhere, I gripped the steering wheel and prepared to steer my car into a tree. I'd even squeezed the accelerator with my foot, hoping if I could just find the courage to see this through then the end would come quickly for me.

It was a bleak and desperate time. I wanted to spare Angela the pain of seeing me in this spiral. At the same time, she was the reason that I couldn't do it. I'd make a split-second decision to bail from every suicide bid and emerge in shock at the wretch I'd become. I never opened up to her about how close I was coming to ending it all, but to this day, I still wonder whether she had worked it out for herself. Because at a time when I could see no other way out, one day my wife quite literally showed me that I still had a future.

'Kerry, we're out of milk. Would you pop out and get some?'

'*What?*'

I was sitting in the kitchen at the time, feeling sorry for myself. Sometimes I could stew in silence for hours on end, as I had been that morning. Angela was at the fridge, having made us both cups of tea. She held a carton in one hand, which she shook to show me it was pretty much empty.

'I can't go out,' I blustered, still surprised that she had even asked me. It was as if she had just suggested I fly to the moon. The fact was I hadn't left the house in ages. 'Angela, look at me!'

'It's just around the corner,' she said. 'What's the worst that can happen?'

Our local store is a two-minute walk from the house. Open all hours, it has always been really handy if we've forgotten something on our weekly supermarket shop. At a brisk pace, prior to the accident, I could be there and back in a matter of minutes. Just then, with Angela waiting for my response, I found myself struggling to find a good reason not to go.

'Oh, come on,' I said. 'One wrong step down a slope or off a curb and I'll be in agony.'

'Then go carefully.'

'What if I stumble and fall?'

'Kerry, it'll be fine.'

'I might panic,' I said, running out of reasons now. 'I really don't think I should be doing this.'

'Take your phone and if you need me, just call.' Calmly, she closed the fridge door. 'I can be with you in under a minute.'

My wife had it all covered. She knew I'd react in this way and patiently addressed every concern I could come up with. Outside, the sun was breaking through clouds in spokes of light.

'Okay,' I said warily, and took a moment to climb to my feet. 'I'll be back.'

It had been months since I'd left the front door and done anything other than shuffle to the car in the street. On the pavement, as I made my way towards the corner, I just felt horribly vulnerable. My breathing quickened as I placed one foot in front of the other. I had some loose change in my pocket. It jangled with every other laboured footstep, reminding me of a funeral toll. I had lived here for decades, yet just then everything looked completely alien to me. I felt as if people were watching me from behind their curtains, though I saw nobody. When an old lady approached, rattling one of those trolley bags on wheels, I hugged a low wall – I just couldn't bear the thought of being knocked in any way in case it sent my back into spasms. She smiled on passing and shared a comment about the weather shaping up. All I could do was acknowledge her gaze and hope my breathing didn't trigger a full-scale anxiety attack. I felt increasingly dizzy and unstable on my feet, but I wasn't going to let this beat me. Instead, I remained at the wall as she passed and waited there for a moment to compose myself. Then, to the fading rattle and squeak from the trolley-bag wheels, I faced the far end of the street and steeled myself to push on. Having come this far, just yards from the path to my door, I couldn't turn around and head home empty-handed.

'I did it!' That was the first thing Angela heard before I closed the front door behind me. 'I made it all the way!'

My wife appeared at the top of the stairs, saw me clutching a pint of milk victoriously, and pressed a finger to her lips.

'I'm with a customer now,' she said. 'But that's nice, Kerry. Well done.'

We shared a smile, and I knew that had she not been cutting hair at the time, then Angela would have danced down those stairs to celebrate with me. This was a big deal. A breakthrough that would not have seemed possible to me for such a long time. I had pushed on to the corner store, holding my phone in one hand in case I needed to call my wife in an emergency. Inside, the store owner had greeted me like the return of some distant wanderer and that had buoyed my spirits as I found the milk we needed, paid at the counter and embarked on the journey home. I'd found the return to be exhausting, and again, I'd had to stop to calm myself down or let people pass. I was braced for that whip crack of nerve pain to stop me in my tracks. After all, I had lived with it for long enough to know that the slightest twitch of a muscle could trigger it. As a result, I only truly breathed freely as I stood in the hallway facing up to my wife. I may have doubted I could do it, but she knew: Angela understood me better than any doctor, it seemed to me just then.

'Don't you want that cup of tea?' I asked.

'I expect it's gone cold now,' she said, before returning to her salon. 'But it didn't go to waste.'

12

Small Steps

ANGELA DIDN'T NEED TO PERSUADE ME to return to the store the next day, or the day after that. I had come back from my first outing for milk on such a high that I quickly started to crave both the challenge and sense of achievement. It was never easy, and several times while out in the street I was struck by intense shooting pains. Instead of letting panic get the better of me, however, I didn't call her. I just reminded myself that this moment would pass and tried to breathe through the worst of it. No matter how bad things could get, I became determined to run a simple errand.

As a result, learning to live with pain rather than be fearful of it, my world expanded from my home to a handful of surrounding roads. It wasn't much, but it helped to break up my day. Instead of counting down the hours until I could take another dose of pills, I'd assemble a list of things we probably didn't need that urgently, like a new washing-up brush or another book of stamps, and head off to the store. In my mind, it was a way of contributing to the running of the household. I knew it was a token effort, but I was desperate to support my wife and feel like I was doing something useful. Getting out meant I also came into contact with my neighbours once again, as well as people who used the store on a regular basis. I'd say hello and sometimes stop and chat. Just hearing my voice outside of my own thoughts was so refreshing. I'm also not the sort of person to list my complaints when anyone asked how I was getting on. Instead, I'd set my personal troubles to one side and that helped put me in a more positive frame of mind.

Physically, this short daily walk reminded me how unfit I had become. For someone who once set out on 60-mile bike rides for fun, this proved quite a wake-up call. I'd resigned myself to the fact that I was unlikely to get back in the saddle again, but hated finding myself out of breath before I'd even reached the junction at the end of our street. What I loved, I discovered, was the fresh air. I'd been trapped in the house for so long, just feeling a breeze on my face was a revelation. It was hard to feel miserable about myself on stepping out into the sunshine. Even the rain was cleansing, having been cooped up inside and so with every trip I made, I found my spirits brightening.

My ritual trip to the corner shop was not some kind of miracle cure for my troubles, but I found it more effective than any medicine. Slowly, things I had previously written off as impossible began to seem like challenges I could take on. If I could manage a short walk then perhaps I could also pop out to post some letters, or cross the road to drop in on a neighbour I hadn't seen in ages. It also encouraged me to look beyond the next round of medication, as I hadn't done for so long, and ask myself what I could do with my life. Just as cycling was beyond my limits, the prospect of going back into the kind of work I used to do was out of the question. I was still in a lot of pain, and though I was learning to manage it, I knew I couldn't sit at a desk.

'Maybe you should think about something you've always wanted to do,' Angela suggested one time, 'a childhood ambition!'

'Well, I liked burning things in the woods,' I said jokingly. 'That's hardly a career move.'

We shared a smile, but it got me thinking. The situation with my back ruled out so many possibilities. Even so, I had inched beyond feeling so despairing that I saw no future for myself. There had to be something useful I could do. I had successfully taken on the challenge of walking around the block, and was actively building on that to rebuild my strength. Now I needed to reclaim my confidence and find work that would help me to feel human once more. It was a question I kept turning over and over in my mind. I wanted to be closer to home and responsible for my own time. I'd also had enough of pushing pens and inputting numbers into spreadsheets. With Angela's comment on my mind, I started considering things I might actually enjoy. While forestry or land management were out of the question, I was still drawn to the idea of doing something practical. For a while, I considered retraining as a driving instructor. I liked the idea of touring around the Lakes again as I had in my early days as a salesman. Then I imagined how my back would react to an emergency stop and that put paid to the idea. Still, Angela had sown the seed. I didn't want to run before I could walk and so, quite literally, I focused on expanding my horizons on foot first.

Rather than confine myself to the block, which I could now manage comfortably, I started taking longer routes to the store. I didn't go crazy – I wasn't strong enough to go striding around Keswick. It was just a question of taking in a few extra roads and feeling like I had reclaimed a little bit more of my life. It had taken nearly two years since the accident for me to think and act positively, and though it wasn't much, I just continued to build on it.

My daily walks, my outlook on life and hopes to return to work all contributed to a sense that I had another chance at life here. Things were very different now, I realised, but rather than sit indoors feeling sorry for myself, I considered each passing day to be another step on my recovery. I also felt better for reducing my medication. So, when I next checked in to see my doctor, I felt ready to get to the surgery under my own steam rather than make the short journey by car.

I wanted to sit down in front of my GP and say that I had walked all the way. It was a chance for me to show that I was taking responsibility for my situation. So, on the afternoon of the appointment, I set out in good time. It was a little further than I had gone before and I had reached the point where I could no longer avoid a hill. Still, it was nothing too daunting; I knew that I could rest at the surgery. Angela had also offered to pick me up if it proved too much.

It was pleasingly quiet outside, I found, with few cars parked against the pavement and a cat contentedly cleaning its paws in the middle of the road. It reminded me that a lot of people were at work at this time. Normally, that would just make me feel even more excluded from the world. As I was making efforts to rejoin it, I found myself pondering my work options once again. Making my way towards the surgery, mindful of the majestic fells that presided over the town, I wondered whether perhaps I could become a bus tour guide around the Lakes. People from all over the world came here throughout the year. I liked talking to them, loved the region and knew a fair bit about the history of the landscape. I could certainly see myself in the role, yet in my heart I didn't quite feel ready. If people were paying me to lead the way, there could be no opportunity for me to take a break and rest if I needed it. With this in mind, I pocketed the thought. It felt good to be looking ahead rather than gazing inwardly from dawn to dusk, but my confidence remained fragile.

What I needed, I told myself wistfully as I turned up the next street, was some kind of guardian angel.

And that's when I met Max.

I was so lost in thought as I walked along, at first I didn't even notice the dog watching me from a yard. It was only when I heard a whimper that I paused and glanced over my shoulder.

'Hello there,' I said, taking a step back so I could see what had just snagged my attention. In response the dog popped its muzzle through the railings to greet me. 'What's your name, eh?'

The Spaniel, a liver and white Springer, peered up at me. I found myself looking into two soulful brown eyes. I

wanted to crouch down and get on the same level. I just
didn't think my back would allow it, yet keeping my
distance from a dog this keen to greet me felt wrong.
Carefully, grasping a railing to take some of the weight, I
lowered myself so one knee touched the ground. The dog
responded by attempting to lick my face.

'Easy,' I said, chuckling to myself as a wet tongue flapped
across my cheek. 'Let me see your tag.' The railings were
wide enough for me to pinch the metal disc between two
fingers. 'Max,' I said, reading the inscription. 'Pleased to
meet you. I'm Kerry.'

Hearing my voice reminded me how much I used to like
talking to Zak. I'd chat to him through the day, often
putting his expressions or behaviour into words for my
own amusement. It was something I first started as a boy
with our dog, Prince. Back then, I was lost and in need of
a friend. In some ways, since the accident, that feeling had
come back to me. I smiled to myself at how easily I'd fallen
into this on meeting a strange dog. Max was a handsome
young fellow and I guessed he could be no more than three.
He was also somewhat subdued. For a Spaniel, it was
unusual for them not to go completely nuts when someone
showed them attention. This one just continued to look
through the railings as if the next move was down to me,
and I could not take my eyes away from him.

'Well, I must be on my way,' I said eventually, and
glanced up at the house in front of me. The dog had the run
of the yard, with a mat on the doorstep that he went to sit
on with his gaze still on me. For a moment I thought about
knocking, if only to say what a friendly Spaniel they had

here, but thought better of it. I might have become a recluse, out of touch with the world around me, but I hadn't lost it completely. I couldn't even be sure that anyone was home. 'I'll see you around,' I told my new friend, and set off with the strongest sense that he was literally watching my back.

The doctor was delighted by my progress. I was actively trying to reduce my medication to a level that managed the pain but didn't fill my brain with cotton wool. I was commended for walking to the surgery, and showing interest in getting back to the workplace, but also cautioned not to be too ambitious on both fronts. My GP asked if I had any further questions, but just then I could think of none.

From the moment I arrived in the surgery, all I wanted to do was turn around and see Max again.

On my way home, I had to remind myself that there was no point in being impatient. My body wouldn't allow me to move any faster, and one misplaced footstep could set me back months. It was just a yard dog, I reminded myself, yet something about that encounter had touched me. Yes, Max was a Springer, a breed that brought back memories, but this one was just so calm. I had come to live in the grasp of a constant anxiety and yet here was a dog seemingly saying to me, 'What's the problem? Chill out.'

With this in mind, all I wanted to do was look him in the eyes once more and see what story he had to tell.

Upon reaching the street, I felt a strange mix of excitement and stupidity. It was just a dog, I told myself as I approached the railings that contained the yard. Would he even recognise me from earlier? I asked myself. At the last moment, prickling with anticipation, I almost crossed to the pavement opposite. Since the accident, I had spent so much time living with negative thoughts, or just feeling numb, that the sense of excitement seemed like an entirely new experience. Rather than bail, however, I steadied my breathing and drew level with the yard.

'Hey, Max,' I said, peering through the rails. 'Remember me?'

I looked one way and then the other, before taking a step back for a wider view. Instinctively, on seeing the Spaniel was nowhere to be seen, I locked away my disappointment before it could take hold. I could hear activity from inside the house. It might have been a television or people chattering. Whatever the case, with Max absent from the yard I had no choice but to walk on. I only had a few streets to go before I reached home, but just then it felt like a very long way.

Aged two and a half, on the Jager Walk
in Fish Hoek in South Africa.

Fish Hoek beach, taken in 1999 while returning from holiday.

With Zak on Melmerby Moor.

Catch of the day – Zak hoping that I drop it!

Max posing for the camera at Seathwaite in Borrowdale.

Max doing what he does best – jetty jumping!

Max, never without his trusty stick, at
Harrop Tarn above Thirlmere.

Our Head of Security keeping watch in Grasmere.

Paddy, just six weeks old, meeting
Max for the first time.

Max teaching Paddy how to pose on
Castlehead above Derwentwater.

Filming with ITV for *Britain's Favourite Walks: Top 100* on Catbells, overlooking our home town.

Prince Harry's first day in the Lake District in January 2019.

On our way to the Royal Garden Party at
Buckingham Palace, with police escort in tow.

The proudest moment of our lives –
being presented to the Duke and
Duchess of Cambridge.

With the boys, happy as can be.

13

Max and Me

'SORRY,' I SAID TO ANGELA later that day and paused to reclaim my composure, 'just give me a moment.'

I'd been midway through bringing her up to speed on my surgery visit when I felt my throat tighten. At the same time, my eyes turned glossy with tears, which I blinked back before they could fall.

'Whenever you're ready.' She smiled at me. 'So, you met a dog …'

Ever since the accident, I found my emotions had become harder to contain. I had spent my entire life keeping my feelings under lock and key. Growing up in unhappy homes had left me with a need to keep everything contained. It was as if I feared that letting my feelings slip would be my undoing. Whether it was dealing with chronic pain that wore down my defences or spending several years shut away from the world, now I couldn't even tell my wife about a Spaniel that had caught my attention without becoming choked.

'I'm being stupid,' I said, chuckling as I wiped the tears in my eyes away with my hand. 'It's just some dog I met on my walk, he's called Max.'

'Why don't you go back?' Angela suggested. 'I'm sure the owners won't mind if you just want to say hello to him.'

'Maybe,' I said, recovering my composure now, and then grinned at the thought that crossed my mind. 'Ange, do you think I could become a professional dog walker?'

My wife regarded me from across the kitchen table. I was only joking and in fact I'd been flicking through the job vacancies in the local paper when she'd sat down with me after work.

'Do whatever makes you happy,' she said, pausing for a moment. 'Even if it makes you cry.'

There were no vacancies in the paper that were suitable for me. Mostly, I looked to amuse myself or read out the far-fetched ones for Angela. While I could never hope to become a removals man, or work for the fire service, I found my attention drawn to courses offered by the local college. I had never considered retraining until now, but over the next few days I realised that I had an opportunity here. While I was reclaiming my physical and mental health, as well as my independence, I had lost my career. What I faced here was a fresh start. If I was to make the most of this second life, perhaps I needed to equip myself with new skills.

The next day, on my walk to the shop, I decided to take the long route via the street where I met Max. I kept an open mind about whether he'd be there. Also, I had lots on my mind in terms of work and so I treated the extra distance as valuable thinking time. Finding the advert for college courses had really focused my attention – I was excited by the possibilities and content to walk and contemplate my future. The closer I came to the street in question, however, the more I found my thoughts extended no further than the yard where I hoped to find a dog.

This time I had prepared myself to find an empty yard. I was ready to just walk on by and head around for the shop. It was no big deal, I told myself, and then sensed my heart leap when a brown and white snout jutted through the railings as I approached.

'Max!' I said happily as the dog came into view. 'How are you?'

The Spaniel in the yard wagged his tail happily. As I lowered my knee gently to the ground once more, I realised this dog had pretty much been on my mind since our first encounter. It was so lovely to see him for real now and he seemed to recognise me. I made a fuss of him, reaching through the railings to ruffle his coat and pat his head. A moment passed, in fact, before I realised that someone had stepped out of the house behind him.

'This is a smashing dog,' I said to the woman nursing a mug in front of me. 'A real one of a kind.'

'Well, Max certainly likes you,' she said warmly. 'He's a very friendly chap.'

Rising to my feet, I thought I should introduce myself. I explained that I lived a few streets down. She said that she recognised me. When she named a family from a few houses down from mine it seemed we had mutual friends. It wasn't unusual in a small town like ours and put us both at ease. With that connection, I told her that I'd met Max a few days earlier.

'I've had a challenging time lately,' I said as the dog enjoyed the attention I was giving him, 'so little things like this really lift the spirits.'

'Well, you've made a friend,' she said, chuckling as the Spaniel raised a paw as if to request further attention. 'Max doesn't get out as much as he'd like and I dare say it means a lot to him, too.'

I looked up from the dog, scratching him behind one ear at the same time.

'Busy life?'

'I care for my father,' she said and suddenly looked a little emotional. 'Sometimes I don't know where the days go.'

I told her that I'd owned a Spaniel in the past and once struggled to fit his needs around my career. We agreed they could be lively dogs.

'Nowadays, I have more time on my hands than I can fill,' I added.

We both looked at Max, who continued to revel in the attention. When I stopped scratching behind his ear, he lifted his paw to bring me back. I smiled and went in for more. If happiness was an antidote to all my problems, I had found it right here.

'Give Max half a chance and he'll fill all the time you can give him!'

Just then, a thought jumped into my mind. On impulse, without thinking how awkward this might make things, I voiced it out loud.

'I'd be happy to walk him if it helps?' I said. Immediately, I came to regret speaking up. I felt like I had just put the poor woman on the spot. There I was, a relative stranger on the other side of the railings, offering to exercise her dog. Feeling stupid all of a sudden, I rose to my feet and stepped away. 'I should be getting on,' I added and drew breath to say goodbye to them both.

'He likes the churchyard,' she said all of a sudden, which caught me by surprise. I followed her line of sight up the street. St John's was situated in grounds that presided over the surrounding roads. From where we were looking, the spire was visible above the trees. 'You're welcome to take him there.'

I looked back at Max's owner, just to be sure I had heard her correctly.

'Really?' I said, and then cleared my throat. 'I mean, I'd love to! It's probably about as far as I can go, to be honest.'

'Then Max will look after you,' she said cheerily, before asking me to wait a moment.

In the time it took her to fetch his lead from the house, I simply stood and stared at Max. I kept telling myself it was just a dog, yet this felt like a privilege. Max seemed to pick up on the fact that he was about to head out. He switched back to the door of the house, his tail swishing.

'You're very kind,' I said as she returned with the dog circling her.

'You're helping me out,' she smiled, before clipping on his lead and opening up the gate.

Without hesitation, Max trotted out and sniffed at my shoes. I took the lead, thanked her again and then said goodbye before she noticed my eyes were brimming with tears.

It came as no surprise to me that a dog would draw this kind of emotional response. I was just aware that it would look odd to someone who didn't know me. So I set off with Max, barely able to believe what had happened. I hadn't expected anything more than the chance to say hello to him again through the railings. Now, here he was, sharing a pavement with me. Not only that, he didn't pull or drag behind. He just trotted alongside me as if we were setting out together on some grand adventure.

'Don't get your hopes up too high, Max,' I said as we approached the junction and the entrance to the church grounds. 'I'm not the world's quickest dog walker.'

By the time we passed through the church gates, I felt exhausted. It had been a slight climb all the way from Max's house, which was no more than 100 metres back. I turned to look behind me, aware that I had come much further than planned, and sensed the first tendrils of a panic attack begin to wrap around my chest. Instinctively, I reached for the church wall to steady myself. At the same time Max looked up and caught my eye.

'It's okay,' I said, thinking perhaps he had picked up on the moment. I didn't want to distress him in any way. Not that he looked in the least bit concerned. If anything, it seemed to me that I had just voiced what Max was thinking. Everything was alright, I told myself just then, and the tension that had gripped me promptly slackened. I took a breath, just to be sure, and then continued with him up the path. It was so peaceful up here. A groundsman was at work on the rose beds outside the church, but as we walked around to the other side I had just Max and my footsteps for company. A squirrel detected our presence and spiralled up a tree trunk. Max pricked his ears, but remained at my side.

'Can I let you off the lead?' I asked, partly to myself. I hadn't asked his owner, but in the short time we had been together I felt as if I knew this little Spaniel. Max had remained glued to me from the moment we set off, and not because he was an anxious dog. His calming presence had been evident to me all the way here. I just had a sense that if I set him free, he would not leave my side. 'There you go, let's find ourselves somewhere to sit.'

Sure enough, as I led the way towards a bench overlooking the town towards the lake and surrounding fells, Max trotted alongside me. He seemed to share my air of contentment and enjoyment of this quiet moment of freedom. Carefully, with one hand on the back of the bench to support myself, I settled into my seat. As I did so, Max hopped up alongside me. He settled on his rear haunches, panting happily while leaning against me.

I looked across at my new friend. He needed a bath, I thought to myself, and a good brush, but underneath it all was a wonderful dog. We had come as far as I could manage, which was really no distance at all, but Max seemed quite content. He wasn't restless, as I had imagined he'd be, anxious about being out with someone he didn't know or challenging in any way. Having been watching the world through the railings of his yard, I wondered if he was just enjoying the same sense of freedom as me. If anyone understood how I was feeling, I thought to myself, it was this little chap. I sensed him press against me a little more.

I responded in kind and it felt lovely. There was no rush to get back, I decided. We had only been gone for 15 minutes at the most. I could hardly return him home now and claim he'd had a decent walk. With this in mind, I settled into the bench and let the sun bathe my face. It was so peaceful and still up there.

With Max at my side, for the first time in an age I felt free.

It was then, some time in that moment of stillness and contemplation, that things seemed considerably brighter. I sat there thinking about what I could do with my life, a question I had been turning over in my mind for some time, when the answer just fell into place. I was taking in my surroundings, which stretched out beyond a rusty gate, over the rooftops to the wilderness beyond.

'Do you see that?' I said to Max and pointed towards the majestic mountain rise that shouldered the lake shore. 'That's Catbells, it's one of my favourite places. I used to take my bike up there. I just haven't been well enough to get out and about in a long time.'

I paused for a moment and focused back on the gate. Noting the padlock and the ivy that had grown up it, I figured it hadn't been opened in a long time. The way I was feeling just then, however, having reached my limit for the day but determined to push myself further from here on out, I saw my future in front of me.

I knew nothing about the line of work that had come to my mind, but it ticked a lot of boxes. I had always liked taking things apart to see how they functioned and then putting them back together again. Since Angela had encouraged me out of the house, I had also come to appreciate that for all the doors that had closed in on me in recent times there were none that couldn't be reopened. I returned my attention to Max and found him still looking out towards the horizon. It was enough for me to know what I wanted to do.

'One day,' I told him, 'we'll go there for a walk. We'll make it happen. What do you think?'

My voice was enough to draw the dog's attention. Max's shining brown eyes peered back at me, inviting me to read into them whatever I wished.

'I'm glad we're on the same wavelength,' I said to amuse myself, and then offered to take his paw in my hand. 'Shake on it, my friend.'

14

Opening Doors

I knew Angela would be surprised when I pitched her the profession that had come to my mind. She looked at me across the table at supper that evening with her eyebrows hitched high. Even so, she didn't dismiss it out of hand.

'I can do a course,' I said, and showed her what I had found on my smartphone. 'With the right qualifications I can start my own mobile business. I'll be my own boss, Angela. It means I can choose when to work, so I can rest between jobs if I have to. Plus, I'll be out of your hair!'

I had come up with this last reason on my way back from the churchyard with Max. Whatever my wife's response, I thought to myself, this would sell it to her. Angela reached for her glass of water, considering me over the rim as she took a sip.

'When does this course start?' she asked me.

I let a few days pass before I went back to see Max. His owner had invited me to take him out again. As much as I wanted to be outside his yard at first light the morning, I decided it was only right to wait. Angela teased me by asking if I was walking Max or dating him and I laughed with her. The fact was that Spaniel had helped to put me in a positive frame of mind. I had come back down from that bench overlooking the fells thinking despite everything, I still had something to offer. It had felt like the world had left me behind since the accident and it had taken a friendly dog to remind me that I could still catch up. At the heart of it, Max reminded me how it felt to be at peace. After so long in the doldrums it was an incredible feeling. I was so grateful to him, and just wanted to give something back. If that meant taking him out for walks with me while I rebuilt my strength and confidence, then we'd be helping each other.

'Where shall we go today?' I asked my new four-legged friend when we set off for the second time. I planned to go a little further than the church grounds, simply because in my experience with Zak, this breed thrived on exercise. Having driven around fields with my old Springer Spaniel bounding alongside, simply to take the edge off his energy before working him as a gundog, I was keenly aware that Max might need more than another short saunter up the hill. I observed Max with Zak in mind, fully expecting him to spin around with excitement on his lead, or tugging to get going faster than I could manage. Instead, he moved at my pace, snout to the ground and tail swishing merrily. It was plain to me that he possessed exactly the same kind of verve and fizz as any other Springer. I could see it in the enthusiasm with which he switched from one smell on the ground to another. Despite every opportunity for him to unleash his true Spaniel spirit, however, he seemed to place my needs before his own.

'So, I'm going to start a locksmith course in a few weeks from now,' I told him, as we cut through the churchyard and headed for the lane on the other side. 'It would be good to open some doors, right?'

Max responded with a glance over his shoulder at me. I had never come across another breed who gave so much eye contact. It marked them out to me from any other dog and gave them so much character. It was as if Max didn't just register the tone of my voice but somehow understood me, which prompted me to get to my point. 'Anyway, I just thought you should know that I won't be around to walk you while I'm studying, but I'll be back, okay?' I stopped for a moment, not only to gather my strength but because I wanted Max to see that I meant every word. 'That's a promise.'

Outside the building where I would begin my training, having arrived in good time I sat in the car and watched my fellow students arriving. That's when I experienced my first serious wobble. Until then, I'd been excited at the prospect of training to do something new. I'd researched the viability of running a small business as a locksmith, read as widely as I could on the subject and talked to Angela about how this fresh start could be the making of me. I was by no means back to full health, but reasoned that I could choose my own hours in order to balance work and rest. If I over-did it one day, I told her, then I could just take the next day off. I would have nobody to answer to but myself, but now that I had rediscovered my drive this was an opportunity I couldn't ignore. It was only when I watched people breezing in through the main doors that I found I was comparing myself to them and falling short.

'I know about agricultural feeds and grasses,' I muttered to myself while summoning the courage to get out of the car and join them. 'What am I doing here?'

Just finding a seat in the classroom proved to be a massive undertaking for me. I felt foolish and unfit to be there. All manner of memories from my school days came back to haunt me. I could feel a sense of panic rising up in me and just had to force myself to sit down and hope I didn't bail before the facilitator began. I could hear people introducing themselves and making small talk. I just wanted to chat to Max, as I had done almost every day on our walks as I counted down towards this course.

Collecting my new friend had become such a part of my routine that I no longer made arrangements with his owner: if Max was in the yard, she had said that I was welcome to take him with me. It became the high point of my days. We'd set out, a little further than the previous time, and I chatted to him as we trundled along. It was a one-way conversation, of course, but over time, I found myself voicing thoughts and feelings I had previously kept to myself.

Talking to Max became like a therapy for me. I found I could open up in ways I'd never dreamt of doing otherwise. I began to feel so close to him that every now and then I'd call him 'Maximoo' and then just 'Moo'. When people talked to me about my troubles, I could see in their eyes that they found it hard to believe that a road shunt could be responsible for ruining my life over recent years. What Max offered was a listening ear and no judgement. I'd spent years in limbo, waiting for some miracle treatment that might rid me of my back pain, but my injuries seemed both incurable and invisible. From the outside, I looked fine, and that could make things really difficult when trying to make anyone understand what I was going through. It was only as I shared my experience with Max, putting all the thoughts I'd stored up over time into words, that I truly came to appreciate how damaging this had been for my mental wellbeing. That I had come seriously close to taking my own life was an unbearable reality for me to process. It seemed unthinkable now. I was still living with discomfort and pain, of course. I was just learning to come to terms with it. Outside, in the open air, I didn't feel like it dominated me. I had Max as my sounding board. He was there to keep me company and guide me, as well as set me thinking about how I might sneak him home for a bath because he'd rolled in fox poo. I was just reflecting on this in the classroom, in fact, when a voice at the front called for everyone's attention.

Five minutes into the course, as the facilitator took us through the principles of locksmithing, I was hooked. All my nerves and reservations just fell away as I listened to him introduce the subject. Later, when he handed out a door lock mechanism to each of us, along with a set of picking tools, I couldn't wait to get stuck in. Before he'd returned to the board in order to take us through the disassembly process, I had taken mine apart. I was so hungry to learn that I sat with the lecturers through lunch breaks and used my spare time putting everything I had learned into practice. At the same time, I began to look ahead to the day that I qualified. I started buying the tools of the trade and then took the plunge and purchased a van. This was a big deal for us financially and committed me to making the venture work. I was excited and scared in equal measure, but determined to move on with my life. It was a blessing to have Angela's full support and she shared my delight when I qualified. As for Max, I kept him fully informed of progress at every opportunity I had to walk with him.

'I'm going to put out some leaflets,' I said on the day that I received my formal certification. 'I was wondering if you'd like to help me deliver them? I thought we could do a couple of roads each day and see what kind of response we get.'

As well as being a plan of action to get the business off the ground, it also allowed me to spend more time with Max. I plotted out a delivery route across town. It would take us a week to cover and took us on new walking circuits. Sometimes people would catch me as I popped a leaflet through their door and I'd stop and chat about my services. As I did so, I'd notice their attention turning to the dog at my side. Some would crouch and pet Max, or comment on his lovely manner. Eventually, I stopped saying I'd just borrowed him and simply agreed that he was indeed one of a kind.

By the time we had posted the last leaflet through a door, I was both exhausted and elated.

'I couldn't have done it without you,' I said to Max as we made our way back to his house, and I meant it. The task of visiting every house on a street, often bending down to find a letterbox, had caused my back to unleash hell on me. It had triggered shooting pains and spasms, but no matter how bad it got, I knew it couldn't kill me. I just had to relax through the worst of it, which meant focusing on Max so I didn't tense my body.

And each time that moment passed, I felt a little stronger.

After dropping off Max, I returned home feeling like I had given my career the best possible start.

'The good people of Keswick know who to call now,' I said to Angela, and placed my mobile on the table like some religious artefact. 'As soon as someone has a problem with their locks, just watch that phone light up.'

'You did put the right number on the leaflet?' she asked me, having contemplated the silent mobile for a moment.

'Very good,' I said, and waited until she headed upstairs before I unfolded one I had left in my pocket and checked just to be sure.

The next day, with no calls to my mobile, I began to worry. Had I made some terrible mistake? I'd done my research and no other mobile locksmith operated in the area. Surely someone in this town would need my services, I thought to myself. I found myself pacing the kitchen and the living room, willing the phone to ring. Slowly, I sensed my anxiety rising. It felt like the air supply was running out in the house, which was when I decided the best thing I could do would be to take myself outside for a walk. With my phone in my pocket, having checked I hadn't accidentally flicked it onto silent, I set off to find myself some respite.

'What would you do?' I asked from our churchyard bench. Beside me, leaning in so close I could feel his body warmth, Max surveyed the vista beyond. 'I suppose we could keep on leafleting, but I can't help thinking this has been a big mistake.' Max licked his chops. He didn't look like he had any regrets. I pulled out my phone. Sighing to myself, I checked the home screen and then looked over the jumble of rooftops beyond at the lake and steep wooded hillsides.

'Maybe this is as far as I'm supposed to go,' I said to myself.

For a minute we just sat and admired the view. It was impossible to feel too down in the face of such a spectacular vista. Even so, I knew we couldn't stay here for ever. At some point, I would have to take Max home and face up to reality. Max showed no sign of restlessness. In fact, he switched from sitting beside me to curling up with his muzzle on my lap. It was so comforting to have him with me. We hadn't known each other for long and yet I couldn't imagine what life would be like without him. Drawing strength from his presence, I told myself it was time to go back down the hill and begin to deal with the situation. Angela would understand. She knew I enrolled on that course with the very best of intentions and it had given me an opportunity to focus on my future. I could only think that other locksmiths were covering the market from further afield and I had simply overlooked their existence. We could sell the van, I told myself as we left the church yard and crossed the road. Yes, there would be some financial loss, but the experience had been worthwhile. It proved to me that I was capable of moving on with my life and I had Max to thank for that.

'I might not be a locksmith,' I said on reaching his road, 'but I promise you we'll visit Catbells very soon.'

I had grown familiar enough with Max to know that he would look at me every time he heard my voice. I adored this connection – it just helped me feel like we could face anything together. Then my phone, which I had forgotten I was carrying, rang. In fact, it took me a moment to find what pocket it was hiding in.

'Hello,' I said, not recognising the number on the screen. 'Yes … yes, this is a good time.' I glanced at Max, and then grinned from ear to ear. 'That's right, the locksmith. How can I help you?'

15

The Head of Security

WITHIN A MONTH of taking my first booking, I had enough
work to know that I had made the right decision. It seemed
like one job led to another, and I seized every opportunity
to work to the highest standard. As a locksmith, I found
every job was different. From the client to the challenge, I
got to meet new people and combine problem-solving with
practical skills. It was a far cry from sitting at a desk from
nine to five, and as word spread about my business so I
found myself on call-outs beyond Keswick.

Travelling around in the van was the best bit. It was like
my mobile office and a cocoon from the rest of the world.
The accident had left me wary of other drivers and so I
preferred to take quieter routes that were often also more
scenic. So, rather than barrel along a bypass, I might find
myself winding up country lanes that overlooked lakes,
forests, meadows and valleys. Sometimes I would pull over,
spin open my flask and enjoy a cup of tea with panoramic
views. After decades as a salesman, a career in which
managing pressure and stress was all part of the package, I
had found a new profession and I loved it. If my back

played up, it didn't defeat me – I just built some downtime into my schedule and put my health first.

This wasn't a life I had ever foreseen, but I loved it. I was in work that I found fulfilling and meant I was able to spend more time with Angela. We even started going out for lunch together during the week. We would drive out to a cafe in Portinscale, overlooking the lake and the fells beyond, and spend an hour catching up with each other. It became a regular way for us to divide our days and just one more feature of a new life that I hadn't considered possible. And at the heart of it all, within weeks of starting up as a locksmith, was a Springer Spaniel called Max.

'I was wondering,' I said to his owner one day, having parked the van outside my house and then walked up to see Max, 'would it be possible for me to bring him with me to work tomorrow?'

I had come to know Max's owner a little bit since meeting her. I knew she was very busy and seemed grateful that I was happy to take him out with me on walks. I wasn't sure how she would react to this suggestion, however, as it meant that Max would be away for much of the day.

'Well, it's an interesting idea,' she said, watching Max as he presented me with a tennis ball from a corner of the yard.

In that moment, I felt a stab of anxiety. It was the same whenever I approached the house and worried that he might be out. It was as if Max had given me a taste of how it felt to be normal and without him, I might lose that. Just then, waiting for his owner to make a decision, I felt like a little dream I'd been contemplating was set to come crashing down.

'If it's too much then I understand,' I said, and tried to sound upbeat. 'I just thought he might like to ride in the van.'

Max's owner switched her attention to me. At the same time, Max dropped the ball at my feet as if hoping I might play a game with him. Then she beamed broadly.

'Spaniels are working dogs, aren't they?'

'Yes, they are,' I said, smiling with her. 'But I don't think Max will be much good with a screwdriver. I was thinking he could just keep me company on the road.'

'What do you think, Max?' she asked. 'Maybe you could guard the van while Kerry is on a job?'

Max nosed the ball a little closer to my feet, as if to remind me what was important here.

'I can offer you a job title as part of the package,' I said to him. 'Head of security, what do you think?'

Scooping the tennis ball from the ground, I bounced it in the air for him. Max caught it effortlessly between his jaws.

On our first outing, I opened up the rear doors of my van to load up my tools. Max stood beside me, watching intently, but showed no sign of wanting to jump in. Then I headed around to the passenger door so I could drop my lunchbox in the floor well and he hopped up onto the seat.

'My right-hand man,' I said, though technically he was on the left. Still, it suited me. 'Let's go!'

Our first call-out took us to a house on the other side of Keswick. After parking on the road, I kept the windows ajar so the interior stayed cool and ventilated, but worried that Max might wonder where I'd gone. I was working inside the house and kept popping back to the front window to check on him. Every time I would peep out and see a Spaniel sitting upright with his gaze on the pavement ahead. He was completely calm and looked quite content. It was only a quick job. When I'd finished, and climbed back behind the wheel, Max looked across at me as if expecting a report.

'That's one happy customer,' I said. 'Shall we find somewhere for a walk before the next job?'

The great thing about living in a town within the Lake District is that the wilderness is only minutes away. We just had to jump in the van, drive up the hill out of Keswick and the fells were our playground. I had no need to walk Max on a lead and this is where he came alive. He would bound off into the heather, overjoyed at the sense of freedom, but all I had to do was call his name and he would snap back to my side. To begin with our little walks would last for a matter of minutes. I was well aware of my limitations and anxious not to compromise my ability to work. Of course, Max would cover about four times the distance I had managed in the same time and so I never felt as if I was holding him back. If anything, I came to consider us to be working partners with a shared love of the outdoors and a service to provide to the community.

With every week and month that passed, I found demand picked up. I put my health first and took time out when I needed it, but remained determined to make a success of my fledgling career as a locksmith. I even started a Facebook page for the business, thinking perhaps people nowadays would look online for local services. Much of my work came from word of mouth, which was great, and I found that word spread online in the same way. I always tried to do my very best, and with a smile on my face. In return, customers felt moved to recommend me.

As my phone continued to ring with call-outs, I found myself attending jobs beyond Keswick. It was so nice to have Max alongside me. He clearly enjoyed coming along for the ride as much as the exercise in between call-outs and being spoiled by the cafe staff when I joined Angela for lunch. Whenever we returned to the van, he would sit there waiting for me to belt him in and then watch the road as closely as me. Max also proved to be a calming presence when I was driving. The accident had affected every aspect of my attitude to other road users. Quite simply, I came to consider every car and lorry as potential killers. If anyone drove too close behind, I could become quite stressed. I'd glance repeatedly in my rear-view mirror and mutter at them to back off. I can only think that Max learned to pick up on the tone because on those occasions where I could become animated, he'd rest a paw on my arm as if to say, 'Chill out, just let them pass.' It worked as well, because I'd pull over so they could speed on their way and in a flash, all the tension would just leave me. Without Max at my side, I know that I would have tightened my grip on the wheel and got into some potential road-rage incident. He made a difference to my life, I realised. Not only did I need him in the passenger seat in order to feel comfortable about driving, I relied on him for companionship, a chance to talk and get back in touch with outdoor life. He even came to join Angela and I for lunch and would sit quietly under my seat while I caught up with my wife. Life was good and Max helped to make it complete.

Gradually, our walks in between jobs increased in distance. I still moved ponderously, anxious not to provoke my back, but would set my sights on a ridge or gate a little further afield than we had gone before. Max thrived on the extra time outdoors, of course, and I loved to watch him in his element. As a Springer, he seemed to embody a sheer joy for life. In particular, I learned that he had a passion for sticks. As soon as he launched from the van, his first mission was to root around beneath tree canopies for something suitable he could clamp between his jaws, even if it was basically a fallen branch, and that's where it would remain for the duration of our walk. He was always so proud of his find and would trot along with his head held high, no matter how broad the stick. We often followed a path that wasn't wide enough for his prize possession, but Max would find a way. With his stick balanced like a tightrope walker's pole, he'd sway from one side to the other to negotiate anything from a stile to a narrow bridge across a stream. It was comical at times, but his commitment to the cause was admirable and a measure of how loyal he could be. I only had to look at the way he related to me to recognise this. From the moment he left the confines of his yard, I wasn't so much his master but a partner in adventure. We relied on each other. What's more, as I established my work as a locksmith in the area, I found that Max became central to my business.

*   *   *

'How are you?' I asked a letting agent who had become a regular customer. I had just dropped off a new set of keys for a lock installed in one of her properties.

'I'm good,' she said simply and I watched her gaze extend over my shoulder to the dog waiting in the van outside. 'How is Max?'

It was the same wherever I went. Anyone who knew me was aware that I had a very special Spaniel in tow and that was the focus for their attention. Frankly, I was happy to let the spotlight shine on him. Max could make people smile on a miserable Monday morning and that included me. It reached a point where people would call me because they'd locked themselves out of their house and then ask for me to bring Max so they could hang out with him while I worked. Although I had left behind my career as an agricultural salesperson, I was aware that Max gave my business a distinctive profile: I was the locksmith with the dog. Wherever I went, my four-legged head of security would accompany me and if that brought in more work, neither of us could complain. It just meant more time on the road, out walking in the countryside, and the chance to be together.

For all the good times we shared, however, there was one daily event that I came to dread.

'Here we are, Moo. Back home, safe and sound. I'll see you tomorrow, okay?'

I only had to look at his body language as I shut the yard gate behind him to know that Max felt the same way as me. It was horrible. I didn't want to leave him behind and he looked at me as if perhaps I wasn't coming back. All I could do was try to sound as upbeat as possible, especially if his owner had come out to see me. It wasn't fair to show what a bond we had built and yet I'd walk away feeling miserable. I couldn't hide it from Angela, however, who picked me up on it one day after work.

'You're a different person with Max,' she observed. 'It's like that dog brings out the best in you.'

'He does in a way,' I admitted. 'It's a shame you can't come and work with us so we can share it with you too.'

Angela raised her hand to stop me there.

'I'm not getting in that van of yours,' she declared. 'It's covered in dog hair!'

We shared a smile. I promised to clean the interior.

'It's my happy place,' I said by way of explanation and then remembered that I had taken a picture of Max earlier on my phone that I had wanted Angela to see. I dug my mobile from my pocket and found the shot. There he was in his seat, the window down behind him, one paw resting on the edge like some long-haul trucker. 'Isn't that great?'

'It's a smashing photograph,' she said. 'You're good at taking pictures of him. Maybe you should share some on your Facebook page.'

'Angela, if anyone's going to check out that page they'll expect to see pictures of locks, not a Springer Spaniel.'

My wife still had my phone in hand. She closed the photograph and brought up the page in question. Watching her scroll through the pictures I had posted, which even I conceded were dull, it was no surprise to see her frowning. There was only so many times I could photograph a lock in bits before people began to unfollow me.

'Max might liven it up,' she said, handing me the phone back. 'Even I might give it a like.'

I've always enjoyed taking pictures. I don't consider myself to be a natural-born photographer, but I do like to compose my shots carefully. At weddings, I'm the kind of guy who spends a while making sure that everyone is assembled so that nobody is obscured from view. The results may never hang in a gallery, but I can generally say that I've given it my best effort. Meeting Max, I found myself frequently firing up the camera on my phone. He had such a noble, soulful look at times, and that's what I set out to capture. It helped that we live in one of the most beautiful regions of the country. On walks, it was easy to find an epic backdrop of forested hillside flanks or rugged boulders, while Max proved himself to be a natural model. He would sit or stand on request, but mostly, I liked to capture him unawares. If I was lucky, I could grab a shot of him shaking his coat with his face in focus and his chops in washing machine mode. Those kinds of pictures made me smile, but I wasn't sure they struck the right tone for my Facebook page. Instead, I started taking pictures of Max in the van or beside it and then captioning each upload to chart the average day in the life of my head of security.

We are in Borrowdale this morning, I would write, along with a picture of Max peering over the dashboard, before uploading the shot and then getting on with a job. Later that morning, I would check the page to find a handful of likes and comments about my sole employee looking hand-some. It would inspire me to take another picture of him sitting beside my van, with my business logo visible on the side, drawing yet more thumbs up. It was fun, I discovered, but within a short space of time, I found myself bending my own rules about what was suitable for my locksmith page.

Enjoying an ice cream in Buttermere with my head of security, was the kind of thing I began to upload over the following weeks. Strictly speaking, it had nothing to do with work, but the response brought people to my page. Sometimes it would earn me enquiries about my services and that could lead to jobs. It didn't take me long to realise that being creative with my pictures of Max, as I did for fun, could generate more interest in my services. So, having started out with formal portraits that were basically product placements, I found myself plotting new and inventive shots as we travelled between jobs. Eventually, I felt no need to keep framing Max as a locksmith's dog and just took pictures of him out on the hillsides, where he was in his element. Max seemed to enjoy himself in front of the camera as much as I enjoyed being behind it. Together, we had found a way to make my business grow and it really didn't feel like work.

16

Lost and Found

FINISHING WORK EARLY ONE DAY, I decided to take Max on a walk I had promised him on our first outing to the churchyard.

'What do you think?' I asked from a windswept viewpoint I used to visit frequently before the accident. Catbells offered a magnificent view of Derwentwater and her islands, including one with an eighteenth-century house that belonged to the National Trust. I hadn't been to this spot for a few years. As always, I found myself looking down at that grand house and grounds, wondering how it must feel to be so cut off from the world. Back then, I could only imagine. Now, however, I felt relieved to be on this side of the water.

'It's a good feeling, right?'

I looked around for Max and then smiled to myself. While I had been trying to spot the church over in Keswick to the north, he had headed down the slope beside me. I watched him exit from a pocket of trees before picking his way towards me, carrying a stick wider than he was long.

'You can leave it beside the van,' I chuckled and turned for the short walk down the path to where I had parked. 'But we'll have to leave it here for another day, maybe even tomorrow if the weather holds.'

On the day that I had walked Max to the churchyard, the prospect of visiting my favourite local fell had seemed like a distant dream. It hadn't been easy, picking my way up the path from the bridge that crossed the stream, and then hiking to the outcrop overlooking the lake. Still, it was just one more little achievement, and drove my appetite to take on bigger challenges. By pushing my boundaries in this way, I was rediscovering the world but this time seeing things in a new light. I didn't feel like I had to do it all on my own any more, and for that I had Max to thank.

Our drive home was nice and relaxed, but a little sad as always. For all the time we spent together, it still felt like a wrench to drop Max back at the yard. While I fully recognised that this was where he belonged, there was nothing I could do to stop the feeling of emptiness that accompanied me back to my own house. Sometimes as I left, even Max would look at me as if to ask what was going on. 'Hey, we're having a good time here!' I imagined he would say. 'Why stop now?'

On this particular afternoon, as I pulled up outside the house, Max's owner came out to see me. I greeted her at the gate and shared the highpoints from our day.

'He should be worn out,' I said and told her we'd just come down from Catbells.

'That's nice,' she said, but from her tone I could tell she

had other matters on her mind. 'Kerry, there's something I need you to know.'

'What's up?' I asked, mindful of the unease in her voice.

'We're moving.'

'What?' I took a step back in surprise. 'To where?'

'We're leaving Keswick,' she said and then shrugged apologetically. 'New job and new start.'

'Well … congratulations,' I said. 'That's great news.'

Max's owner offered me a sympathetic smile. She knew, without putting it into words, what this meant to me.

'I'm sorry,' she said and then picked up her tone. 'We're leaving at the end of the month, so there's plenty of time for you two to say goodbye.'

That evening, when Angela asked me what was on my mind, I could barely put it into words. I was completely shocked by the news. Just as I had met a dog that transformed my life, so it seemed our friendship was about to end.

'It's not for another few weeks,' she reasoned with me. 'And Kerry, you could always get a dog of your own.'

'But it won't be Max,' I protested. 'No other dog is like him.'

Max joined me for work the next day as usual. We set off for a job and I found myself conducting my usual one-way conversation. Only this time, as he listened from the passenger seat, I opened up about just how much he meant to me. By the time we arrived, I was struggling to hold back tears. While it was lovely to have him at my side, it also reminded me that our time together was nearly up, so I set out to make the most of what we had left.

I took Max to the coast one day and we each ate ice cream on the beach, which had fast become his favourite treat. I also discovered that he had another passion that almost rivalled his love of a good stick: water.

The first time Max leapt into the lake, racing around me on a walk along the wooded shore at the far end of Derwentwater, I worried he'd just got carried away. Did he think the water was solid ground? My concern lasted for about a second until I saw him paddling away happily. I actually had to call for him to come out, which immediately left me feeling like a spoilsport. Having shaken himself back and forth, soaking me in the process, he simply looked at me as if waiting for evidence that there could be anything better in life than that. I had to agree there wasn't much that could rival a good swim – I just wished he had jumped in earlier on our walk.

'Nobody's going to thank me returning a wet dog,' I said, mindful of the time.

With no towel to hand, but a breeze coming across the water, I figured a trot along the shoreline would dry him out. I didn't want to go home, especially not since it felt like we didn't have long left together like this. It made me feel sick just thinking about how life would be without Max. I had no doubt that he had saved me; I just hoped I had given him a chance to enjoy the outdoors before he left.

I was so lost in thought that I didn't even register the boat jetty as we passed it. I saw Max switching back towards me from a distance, which wasn't unusual as he effectively ran around me in a wide spiral as we walked. A moment after he raced by, however, I heard a thunder of paws on planks, a momentary silence and then a big splash.

'For crying out loud, Max!' By the time I turned to face the jetty, he was merrily cutting through the water beyond it like the prow of a ship. 'We can do this tomorrow!'

Max glanced around at me, still paddling along, and then circled back towards the shoreline. Closing in on dry land, I saw the look of sheer joy in his eyes and my impatience faded in favour of a smile. This time I stood well back when he scrambled from the lake and shook his coat, and then chuckled as he sat back on his haunches and looked at me expectantly.

'You want to jump off the jetty again?' I asked him. It had been a long day. My back was beginning to twinge. Even so, I couldn't think of a good reason to say no. Instead, I dug out my phone from my pocket. 'Just let me take a picture this time!'

I kept some rag cloths in the van for work. I found one that hadn't been used to wipe oil from a lock and used that to towel down Max as best I could. Even so, the only thing that would shift the smell of damp dog was a good bath.

'Keep a low profile tonight,' I said, having encouraged him through the gate. 'I'll pick you up in good time tomorrow and you can pop round to mine for a shower, alright?'

'Hey, Kerry! All well?'

I looked up to see Max's owner emerge from the house. Max trotted across to greet her. She cupped his muzzle in both hands, clearly registered the state of him and looked back at me.

'So,' I said to begin, 'we went for a walk down by the lake …'

I had only just begun, but judging by the way she pretended to scold Max it was pretty clear he had form for this kind of thing.

'He does enjoy a swim,' she said, tutting at the soggy Spaniel at her feet.

'I'm sorry,' I said. 'Probably best to keep him away from radiators unless you want the whole house to stink.'

She looked back at Max and then smiled at me.

'He's a state,' she agreed. 'As well as tired and happy. I really can't thank you enough, Kerry. He loves spending time with you.'

'Well, I'm going to miss him,' I said and stopped there because a catch had suddenly formed in my throat. By now, sensing supper was at hand no doubt, Max had slipped indoors. It left me with nowhere else to look but at his owner.

'This move,' she said, 'it's a shame you can't come with us. I'm going to be so busy that Max will have to get used to a lot more time alone.'

I nodded, sinking my hands into my coat pockets. I wasn't ready for a conversation about something I was dreading and so I told her I needed to be off home.

'Owning a dog is quite a commitment,' was all I could say, retreating towards the van. 'But I'm sure you'll find a way.'

* * *

As ever, Angela could pretty much read my manner when I walked through the door enough to know how my day had gone.

'Something's got you down?' she said. 'Tricky customer?'

'All my customers are great,' I said as I hung my coat on the hook. 'It's Max.'

Angela waited for me to face her.

'I'm sorry,' she said. 'Even though they're leaving, nothing will take away how much he means to you.'

I told her about the exchange with his owner. At the gate, when I listened to her concerns about moving, I remembered how it had changed things for Zak and me. I had uprooted our lives for my career and my poor dog paid the price. Working all hours, I'd been forced to leave him in the care of friendly neighbours. That this marked the end of his life still left me feeling bad, as I explained to Angela.

'I just wish Max could stay,' I said. 'I can give him everything he needs, just as he gives everything to me.'

'Then why don't you offer?' Angela's suggestion was followed by silence. I simply stared at her, trying to process what she had just said.

'You mean, ask if Max can live with us? Angela, I can't do that!'

'Kerry,' she said simply, 'what have you got to lose?'

17

Stay with Me

IT TOOK ME A FEW DAYS to summon the courage to talk to Max's owner. Angela had given me a glimmer of hope, I just didn't want to pin everything on it. I needed to be prepared for disappointment, because in my mind this was a doomed proposition.

In that time, I focused on having fun with Max. He waited patiently for me on jobs and then we headed out on walks together. I had my phone camera with me at all times, while Max made the most of being a canine model. Whether he was looking out towards the horizon from a hilltop, bounding madly along a muddy path or jumping for a stick I had thrown him, it was a joy to capture his true nature.

I was also discovering that more and more people felt the same way as I did about him. Every time I uploaded a picture to my business page on Facebook, I'd watch the likes and shares begin to tick over. I also received nice comments about Max or queries about the location. It made me realise that a lot of the interest was coming from beyond the local area. It seemed a bit pointless advertising my locksmith services outside Keswick and the surrounding villages, but then it was such a buzz to see that I wasn't alone in recognising what a wonderful dog I had at my side.

Of course, we returned to the jetty. I just went a little earlier in the day so that Max had time to dry out. Watching him charge off the end and into the water made me laugh out loud. Quite literally, it seemed to me, he jumped for joy. Having circled back to shore he'd keep going back for more until it was time to leave. Whatever little adventure we got up to in between jobs, I just didn't want it to end.

Eventually, one afternoon having finished our day with a walk to a viewpoint across Keswick from a fell called Latrigg, I steeled myself to ask the question that had been on my mind since Angela first suggested it. First, as we pulled up outside the yard, I wanted a word alone with Max.

'Whatever happens,' I said, 'wherever you end up, it's important to know that you are loved. Not just by me, but everyone around you. Do you understand me, Moo?'

Max registered my voice with a plaintive gaze and then switched his attention to the house. His owner had come out to greet us, as she often did. I took a deep breath and climbed out of the van.

'Hello, Max!' she said at the gate, opening it up for him to slip through. 'I hope he hasn't been any trouble for you.'

'None at all,' I said. 'Although as an apprentice locksmith, he has some way to go.'

She laughed, before inviting me in for a cup of tea. On instinct I politely declined, saying that I needed to be getting back. As I did so, a small voice inside me berated my cowardice. I wanted to speak up and put my suggestion to her. Face to face, however, it just seemed so futile.

'So, we have a date for moving out,' she said next. 'We're off in a week.'

'A week?' I blinked in surprise. It seemed like no time at all. 'So soon?'

'We're all set,' she said and then dropped her attention to Max. 'All except for one thing.'

'What's that?' I asked, still reeling from the news. All of a sudden, I found Max's owner considering me with an air of hesitation. 'Is there anything I can do to help?'

'Kerry,' she said, 'I want to ask you something, but just want you to know that you can say no and we'll forget all about it.' She paused there for a heartbeat before drawing breath again. 'I've been thinking things through since our chat, all that talk about dogs being a commitment.'

'Yes?'

'When we leave Keswick, would you like to keep Max?'

For a moment, I struggled to process everything she'd just said. There I'd stood, too meek to raise the same proposition, and she had come out with the very same thing. I cleared my throat to respond, aware that my chest was tightening with emotion.

'Well, I'm sure it's something I can talk over with my wife,' I said and hurriedly blinked back tears. 'Let me ask her and I'll get back to you tomorrow.'

Later that evening, when I finally regained control of my emotions to tell Angela what had happened, she looked at me in disbelief.

'What are you like?' she asked finally. 'This is the one thing you've dreamed about and all of a sudden you're not so sure?'

'She took me by surprise!' I reasoned.

'So, you left her hanging.' Angela smiled despite herself. 'What's stopping you from just saying yes?'

'I wanted to discuss it with you,' I reasoned. 'I can't bring Max home without your blessing.'

We had sat down for supper, but I wasn't hungry. Ever since Max's owner had offered to make my dream come true, I'd struggled to believe it could really happen. I'd grown up to believe I didn't deserve to be happy and though I'd left much of that behind on getting married, it was in my bones. Watching my life fall apart after the accident just brought it all to the surface once again and then Max came to the rescue. According to my view of the world, it was only a matter of time before the joy he brought me would come to an end. Now it seemed I had an opportunity to make him a part of my life permanently, I didn't know how to take it all in.

'I know what Max means to you,' said Angela.

'Yeah, but I know you're not mad keen on dogs,' I said.

Angela didn't disagree. 'They just make so much mess,' she said. 'I don't do dog hair or muddy paw prints, and the barking would drive me up the wall.'

I had heard her reasons before. Just listening to her reel them off now, I sensed what hopes I had built as I made sense of the situation begin to evaporate.

'You don't need to go on,' I said. 'I'll let her know in the morning.'

'Why wait until then?' She reached for her glass, signalling for me to do the same. 'You can call her right now and confirm that we'd be delighted if Max came to live with us.'

'But, you—'

'I'll survive.' Angela leaned forward and clinked her glass against mine. 'If it makes you happy, that's fine by me.'

I almost didn't bring Max to work with me the next morning, I was just so emotional and mindful that I would be unable to focus on the jobs I had to do. Then again, I was desperate to see him and also his owner in person. I wanted to talk through the details of taking him on and to assure her that I would do everything in my power to ensure that Max had the best life possible. Before climbing out of the van to greet them both, I had to steel myself but was glad I made the effort because it worked out just fine. It was good to see his owner and be sure she felt that she was doing the right thing.

'I appreciate how hard this must be,' I told her. 'And I want you to know this means the world to me.'

'He's going to have the time of his life,' she said as Max turned circles with excitement at the prospect of jumping in the van. 'We're going to miss him,' she added, 'but I know it's best for Max.'

With a date set for the move, I started to prepare for Max's arrival like an expectant father. I created a space for him to sleep in the room at home I used as an office. I bought a basket and mat, and rifled through the airing cupboard for old blankets and towels. I set up a feeding station in the kitchen and began to acquire balls and toys to keep him occupied.

'He's not a puppy,' said Angela one day, after I returned from yet another trip to the pet shop. 'What is he, five or six years old? Surely, he'll have grown out of toys by now?'

'A dog is forever young at heart,' I said, and set down the bag that contained a range of chews. 'I don't want him to get bored and go off the rails.'

'Well, I'm just glad that Max has got you back on track,' she said with a chuckle. 'After everything we've been through, it seems you've been saved by a Spaniel.'

I couldn't stop counting down the days. Every morning, when Max jumped into the van, I'd update him on what he could expect to find at his new home. I even brought him back with me a couple of times – I wanted him to become familiar with the shape, size and smell of the house. Every time, Max behaved like the perfect guest. Part of me wanted him to go wild with excitement, but then I didn't think Angela would take kindly to it. Instead, he just sniffed around politely and kept a low profile. Increasingly, however, I found that wasn't something he could do so easily when out and about.

'Is that Max?'

The first time it happened, I was loading the van outside the house. Max was standing beside me, inspecting the rear tyres and waiting for me to hurry up so we could be on our way to the next job. 'It is! Look, the Facebook dog, it's Max!'

I turned to see a woman with a buggy cross the road towards us. She didn't live in our street, but judging by the delight on her face it seemed she was familiar with one of us.

'Hello,' I said, if only to be polite, but I'd never seen her before in my life.

Stopping in front of us, she dropped down beside the buggy. The toddler strapped into the seat was staring at Max in wonder.

'This is the doggy from Mummy's phone,' she said and then beamed up at me. 'Your locksmith page,' she said to explain, 'we love your photographs.'

'Thanks,' I said, flattered and equally surprised that anyone would recognise a Spaniel in the street like this. 'You can stroke him if you like? He's very friendly.'

I glanced at Max. He looked up at me and trotted closer when I gave him the nod. The little one in the buggy reached out in delight and touched his muzzle. Max wagged his tail in response.

'He's a delight,' said the mother, rising back onto her feet again. 'We look at your pictures every day. My daughter has even started asking to see them for herself.'

'Really?' I said in amazement. 'Well, that's kind of you to say so. Thanks very much.'

'No, I should thank *you*,' she said insistently. 'It can be hard to get out of the house with a little one. When she's napping, I just like to sit down with a cup of tea and look at Max. Sometimes it feels like I'm out there with you. It means a lot.'

A moment later, with pleasantries exchanged, the young mother and her child were on their way. Even so, what she had told me stayed with me all day. Max hadn't just changed my life, it seemed his gentle manner and love of the great outdoors could impact on others as well.

'You,' I said to him as we motored along later that day, 'are one of a kind.'

I had lowered the window for Max. He liked to pop his snout into the rush of air and though he didn't turn, I watched his gaze flick towards me. We were on our way to our final job of the day, motoring along a country lane, having just been for a stick-throwing session down by a stream. When my phone rang from its cradle on the dashboard, flashing up the name of Max's owner on the screen, I pulled in to take the call on speakerphone.

'There's a problem with the move,' she told me. 'It may not be happening after all.'

As she explained the issue, I simply sat there gazing at some imaginary point beyond the van. I felt sick to the core, but managed to assure her that I understood. Having told me that she would be out later when I returned Max, I asked her to keep me posted and then ended the call.

In silence, with Max at my side, I sat with my phone in my lap. A moment later, with a gasp like the last breath of a man who had fought to stay afloat for so long, I gave in to my emotions.

18

Home

IT WAS ANGELA who kept reminding me that all was not lost. The move hadn't been cancelled, but possibly delayed, and Max's owner was simply being courteous by keeping me informed. That's how she framed it when I came home with eyes rimmed red from weeping.

The news had undoubtedly come as a shock, even though I was hard-wired to be prepared for the worst. What really surprised me, however, was how fragile I was even thinking that Max might not be mine. It made me realise just how central he had become to my life and I worried what would happen to me if the plan for him to move in with us fell apart.

'Just take each day as it comes,' said Angela. 'Enjoy your time together, nothing can take away from that.'

As ever, my wife was right. I took Max with me the next day on a drive across the fells to a customer who had specifically asked me to bring him along. When I arrived, the guy seemed not the least bit concerned about the job he'd asked me to do. Instead, when I rang the bell, he trooped his family out to the van in the drive and introduced them to the 'internet famous dog'.

'It hasn't gone to his head yet,' I joked behind them, but frankly, they weren't very interested in me or anything I had to say.

It was something I chuckled about when we hit the road once more. While it was a nice surprise to find that Max was earning so much attention, I quite enjoyed finding myself out of the spotlight. On several occasions, I had left customers petting Max through the van window while I got on with fixing their locks. It helped to put me in a more positive frame of mind as we followed the road over the pass that led to Keswick.

'The good news is that you can still remain as head of security if you stay,' I told him and then chuckled to myself. 'In fact, I'm not sure the business would be where it is today without you.'

Winding our way back into Keswick, I came to recognise that there was no point stewing over something beyond my control. I felt helpless and desperately wanted Max to join me, but even if that didn't happen, he would still be my colleague and companion when it came to walking the trails and hills. This whole question mark about whether or not he would live with me had made me realise just how dependent on him I had become, but nothing could change the bond we had formed. It was with this in mind that I steered the van into the parking spot outside his house. The emotional upheaval since the call had left me exhausted. I still hated saying goodbye to Max each evening, but I was beginning to get my head around the fact that it was a small price to pay for us to be together through the day.

'Kerry?' Stirring from my thoughts at a tap on my window, I turned to see Max's owner. Then she held up a letter. I had no idea what it was about, but the smile on her face told me enough.

'The move?' I asked, leaping from my seat.

'It's on!' she beamed. 'Everything is back on track.'

Max had just taken the opportunity to scramble across the front seats and drop down onto the pavement.

'Did you hear that?' I asked Max, who must have been fired up by the elation in my voice because he began to dance around me.

'I'm so relieved,' his owner declared. 'It felt as if my life had been on hold.'

'That makes two of us!' I said, because all of a sudden there seemed little point in even trying to play down how much this dog had come to mean to me.

From there on out, I couldn't wait for Max to move in with me. Even so, I kept telling myself that despite everything, there was always a chance that it might not happen. Something had to go wrong and I didn't want my hopes to come crashing down from that high point again. It was hard, but I just tried to enjoy my time with him each day rather than make plans.

By now, my locksmith page on Facebook was earning so much attention because of Max that it seemed rude to try and plug the business. People weren't drawn to updates about lock mechanisms, they wanted to see a Springer

Spaniel romping joyfully across the fells. Through trial and error, I came to realise the photographs that worked best featured Max framed by a wild and rugged landscape that stretched out for miles. As I was blessed to live in a picture-perfect part of the country, I set out on each walk with one eye on potential places for us to get creative with the camera. I felt very lucky. I loved photography, and set myself high standards, and Max was just so natural and biddable that it was one more thing for us to enjoy together. One time up on the hills at sunset, as I lined him up in the viewfinder with a low mist shrouding the lake below, it struck me that I had never felt so at peace with the world. Nothing could change that. As long as Max was at my side, everything would be okay.

I reminded myself of this on the morning of the move. All night, I barely slept a wink – I kept waiting for a text or even a call to say the arrangement had been cancelled. Right up to the moment that I turned into Max's street, to find a removal van outside the house, I fretted that it could still go wrong. There was no sign of Max in the yard. I came close to panicking until I realised that with so much activity between the van and the house he was probably being kept inside. I walked up to the front door, which was open.

With a deep breath, I knocked a couple of times to make my presence known. Max was first to respond. An excited bark from another room and then the sound of approaching footsteps.

'It's only me,' I called in to his owner. 'Your man about a dog.'

One hour later, I closed my own front door behind me and took a moment to compose myself. All of a sudden, this place that had been my refuge and my prison during the worst of times seemed completely different. Why? Because I had just crossed the threshold with a Springer Spaniel at my side and this was his home now.

'Max,' I said, barely able to contain my delight, 'here is where it all begins.'

My eyes were raw from crying, which I had kept in check until we were in the van and on our way. It was tough, no doubt, for his owner and I kept my distance as she said goodbye. Of course, I left her with an open invitation to visit any time and promised I would keep her updated as he settled in. I really did appreciate what a tough decision this must have been for her, but we both had Max's welfare at heart. Just then, as Max sniffed around the hallway, I wondered if he knew what had happened. Judging by his eye contact with me, he certainly seemed aware that I was in an emotional state that day.

'Ange!' I called up the stairs. 'There's someone here who'd like to see you.'

I had to call for her again before she heard me.

'Is it a customer?' she asked, before appearing at the top of the stairs. 'Oh!'

Max trotted to the foot of the stairs, his tail wagging, and then greeted Angela as she skipped down to greet him.

'Isn't it wonderful?' I said. 'I keep having to pinch myself.'

Angela had crouched down beside Max. I watched her lean forward and sniff his coat.

'He could do with a wash,' she said.

'Are you offering?'

'Not in my salon!' she laughed. 'He's your responsibility.'

'I know,' I said proudly. 'And I want to thank you for giving me this opportunity. It means everything to me.'

'I should be thanking Max.' Angela stood back, considering me with a fond smile. 'He's brought you home to me.'

Max padded back to me just then. He sat at my feet and leaned on me, which he had taken to doing whenever I started crying. This time, I chuckled to myself as I sought to regain my composure.

'All this weeping,' I said and wiped my eyes. 'It started when I met him.'

'Well, he's cheaper than a therapist,' said Angela, stepping back up the stairs. 'I need to get back to work,' she told me, 'and you need to call the dog groomer and make an appointment.'

We had a busy day ahead of us and I was glad that I had decided to keep it free from bookings. That morning, the dog groomer gave Max a proper wash and brush up. After taking him for a walk with no mud or water in sight, we then paid a visit to the vet. Max passed the health check, as well as taking his jabs like a trooper. I just wanted to start afresh, tick every box and leave nothing to chance. With all the paperwork to hand, the final act was to get him microchipped. I watched the vet register him alongside my name and address and decided there and then that I had done enough crying for a while.

Naturally, my composure didn't last long. The next time I needed a moment happened soon after we got home that afternoon. Max had come back to the house with me on quite a few occasions in the run-up to this day. So he was familiar with the place. On this occasion, however, I didn't head for the door around four o'clock in order to take him back. Instead, he sat on his bed while I did some paperwork. Every time I glanced over my shoulder, he looked at me expectantly, as if to say, 'Shouldn't we be getting off soon?' Then, as the time approached when we would usually be leaving, he took himself to the front door.

'Max, you can relax,' I told him. 'This is home now and you must be hungry.'

I had supper ready for him. I'd already prepared his bowl on the counter, which I set down beside his water in what would become his little corner of the kitchen floor. Afterwards, we went for a walk just to stretch our legs. It was getting chilly when I came back and so I put the fire on. I don't think Max had ever seen one before, but he liked the heat. With Angela and I in our seats, he lay down in front of it for a while. I watched him doze but never quite drop his guard.

'Bedtime could be interesting,' said Angela as we prepared to turn in ourselves.

'I'll take care of him,' I said, bracing myself for a long night. 'You go ahead.'

For a while after Angela had gone up, I stayed downstairs beside the fire with Max and just stroked him. I still couldn't believe that he was really here and that I was now fully responsible for his welfare.

'It's me and you, Max. From this day forward, we're going to get out and make the most of every day.'

By now, the heat from the fire had helped Max to relax and bask. He stretched and groaned happily. I patted his flank: it was time for bed.

After a quick visit to the garden, I led Max upstairs to my office. His basket was waiting for him and once he had settled, I dropped a blanket over him. I had prepared myself for Max to be a handful, but when I wished him good night and retreated to the door he didn't follow me. He just offered me that soulful look of his that never stops melting my heart and then rested his chin on the edge of his basket.

'Sleep well,' I whispered. 'This is the start of our new life together. We're going to build the business and climb new heights. I want to take you across the fells and beyond, because every time we reach a summit together, it feels like we can still go further.' Slowly, so as not to disturb him or unsettle my back, I rose to my feet. 'Maybe one day, if I'm strong enough, we'll tackle a mountain I've always wanted to climb. Right now, Max, it's a distant dream, but with you at my side, I'll get there, I know it.'

A moment after I clicked the door shut, I heard a small whimper. I stayed quite still, ready to go back in again, should Max become distressed. I stayed as still as I could, hoping he didn't realise I was listening, and even held my breath. On hearing a sigh, and the sound of a tired Springer Spaniel settling in for the night, I crept away and went to bed, and from there on out, I never looked back.

Part Three

19

Beyond Ben Nevis

JUST OVER A YEAR AFTER MAX moved in with me, we took a week off work, packed the van and headed north of the border.

Hiking to the top of Ben Nevis was still a very big deal for me. Even though I had made walking with Max a central part of my life, I continued to live with chronic pain. The only thing that had really improved was my attitude towards it. I had learned to manage the most severe episodes and change my mindset so I no longer felt so trapped. A jolt to my back or misplaced footing would still stop me in my tracks on a regular basis, but I was no longer alone in dealing with it.

Even at the worst moments, I could always reach out for Max, knowing that he would be there for me. He had never let me down in all the time that I had known him and in return, I aimed to give him the best life that I could. The way I saw things, Max had saved me. I could never repay him for that, but became increasingly aware that others saw the qualities in him that had pulled me back from the brink. Throughout the year, I continued to post pictures of my head of security on Facebook. It was clear to me that his appeal now went way beyond my customer base as a locksmith, because I would get comments from people all around the world. Sometimes it was just a compliment about his expression or the scenery, but every now and then I would receive a direct message. Despite the sender being someone I had never met before, often they would open up their heart about issues affecting their lives before thanking Max for making it more bearable. Every time, I felt deeply touched that anyone should reach out in this way and also responsible somehow to make sure that Max connected with anyone who needed him. The surest way to do this, I decided, was to keep on sharing pictures on Facebook that I hoped would brighten lives. Sure, I could post a picture of the van with my contact details on the side, but the fact remained, people came to see a Spaniel with a sheer lust for life.

'Are you ready, Max? On three …'

I stood with my phone camera in one hand and a stick in the other. Naturally, Max's attention was fixed solely on the stick. I would have to be quick as soon as I launched it into the air for him. He would move with lightning speed and live up to his name as a Springer by catching the stick as it sailed through the air.

'… two … one … here we go!'

What I hoped to capture, as both dog and projectile came together, was the building in the background. I always tried to frame my pictures with something interesting behind Max. In general, I made the most of my natural surroundings but on this occasion we were here for work and I had spotted an opportunity for a great shot from the drive.

Business was going well. I received a steady stream of call-outs that kept Max and me on the road, with plenty of time for walks in between jobs. As well as helping customers who had locked themselves out of their homes, businesses or cars, I often found myself invited to become a keyholder for unattended properties. The Lake District is dotted with holiday homes. Sometimes, if the owner wasn't local, they simply wanted to know that someone was watching over their chalet, cottage or shepherd's hut. That meant dropping in to check everything was secure on a regular basis. On this particular visit, however, having caught Max on camera as he sailed back down to earth with the stick clamped in his jaws, I turned my attention to the stately home behind him.

This house and its grounds were open to the public by day. At night, it was unattended. Naturally, the trustees were keen to ensure the building was completely secure. They had recently asked me to upgrade all the locks to meet insurance requirements. It had taken me a week to work my way through all the rooms, as well as checking it all worked with the alarm system, and now I had returned to hand over the keys.

'Is Max working with you today?' asked the security consultant who met me in the grand hallway and served as my contact for the organisation that owned the home.

'He's never off-duty,' I said and gestured over my shoulder. 'Currently guarding the van.'

It was no surprise that one of my customers would show more interest in Max than me and that was fine – it just made work so much more enjoyable.

'You've done an excellent job,' the consultant told me as I took him through the different keys. 'Would you be open to becoming a key holder for us? In an emergency, it would be good to know that we can call upon you.'

'Of course,' I said and told him that I was regularly asked to keep spares for the holiday lets. As well as keeping an eye on the properties, holidaymakers would occasionally mislay a key and I would be on hand to make sure it didn't spoil their fun. My contact from the organisation chuckled at this and then invited me to look around.

'This is a little ... larger scale,' he said. 'Essentially, we'd need you to be on call after hours, should the alarm go off. Not just here but in the other properties in the Northwest that we manage.'

I knew how an alarm system such as this one worked. It was all automated nowadays. If a trip went, it would alert the monitoring centre and they would call the designated key holder. I looked up and around. This was far bigger than a holiday let, as were the other big old piles on the organisation's books. I wasn't afraid of the dark, just mindful of the scale of the undertaking when I had no other staff to help me cover it.

'I'd be happy to take it on,' I said, casting any misgivings from my mind.

My customer looked like he could see straight through me.

'Bring your head of security,' he said with a wink. 'He'll keep you safe and sound.'

Springer Spaniels are known for their love of life. They throw all they have into everything they do, from scoffing their breakfast to barrelling out of the front door to take on the day. Where their reputation falls short, somewhat, is in their capacity to be fierce and intimidating.

'Can you do terrifying?' I asked Max, back in the van. Slipping into the driver's seat, I looked across at my head of security with his tongue lolling from the side of his mouth. 'No, I didn't think so.'

While Max might be the least intimidating dog ever, Spaniels have an incredible capacity to learn. They're very intelligent and need to be kept occupied, which is why they love to pick up new tricks. I had no intention of teaching Max to be aggressive – he didn't have that in his bones. What I could do, I realised, was teach him how to mouse.

The first time I received a call, on a dark and windswept night, I just hoped that Max wouldn't let me down.

'I'm on my way,' I told the operator from the monitoring centre, who had just reported an intruder alarm at one of the organisation's properties at Grasmere. I knew the place well. It was popular with tourists, set in sprawling grounds, and contained a labyrinth of rooms across several floors and wings. If anyone had broken in, I thought to myself, it would be easy to hide from me. This was a job for my head of security.

'Come on, Max,' I whispered, on cracking open the door to my office. 'We might have a rodent problem.'

The drive out to Grasmere took less than 15 minutes. The road out from Keswick was littered with leaves and dead wood that had been blown from the treetops. On pulling into the grounds, the van's headlights floated across the building's facade in front of us. At any point, if I felt at all unsafe, I knew that I could call the police. That was part of the procedure. Essentially, my role was to give the emergency services access to the property. With Max at my side, however, I didn't feel the need to summon help just yet. Instead, on pulling up, I led him to the main door, unlocked it with the master key and then crouched down to make sure he had my full attention.

'You know what to do,' I whispered, braced to open the door. 'Max … *find the mouse!*'

It was a cue that caused his ears to prick. We had been practising this command at every opportunity. It was effectively a game of hide and seek, using balls and sticks or anything that seized his attention. Then, it was just a question of exciting him as he hunted it down until he couldn't contain his bark any longer. As ever, when it comes to training Springer Spaniels, it had proved to be immensely fun and swiftly rewarding. Now, I only had to say the word and Max sparked into life.

'Go, Max. Go …!'

With a gruff woof, as if to acknowledge that he understood, Max rushed through the door as I opened it. I rose to my feet, so relieved to hear him barking as he tore through the ground floor. If there was a prowler present, this would not be a welcome sound. Without a doubt, Max's bark was worse than his bite, which frankly was non-existent, but he sounded like he meant business.

'Find me the mouse, Max! Where's the mouse?'

I switched on the lights in the grand lobby, which immediately made the place less sinister. Max tore up the sweeping staircase, making such a racket had I been creeping around on the rob, I'd already be out on the landing with my hands in the air. He continued to ricochet from one room to another, moving so fast it was hard to keep track of how much of the building he had covered. All I knew was that his presence gave me the confidence to begin sweeping the rooms. I started with the ground floor, still heartened to hear him barking as he thundered around upstairs. It was only when I inspected one of the rooms on that level, however, that I discovered the cause of the alert.

'There!' Max joined me as I directed the torch beam at the open window. The curtain flapped like a loose tongue in the gale and I could feel the rain spots from across the room. A quick check at the ledge told me nobody could have scaled in. The fact that the glass was intact, and the window arm snug on its pin, suggested it had been left open by accident. I closed the window before offering Max a treat from my pocket as a reward for his efforts. 'As my head of security,' I told him, 'it's fair to say you have passed your annual review with flying colours!'

A year into my new life as a mobile locksmith, I could look back on my old career with no sense of loss. I didn't miss the office-bound environment nor the endless drive to meet and exceed sales targets, although I had thrived on it at the time. Now, I considered myself to be a different person and that was someone who could truly say that they were comfortable with life at last. I didn't need to ride a performance road bike 60 miles to feel at peace with the world around me and appreciative of everything it had to offer; I simply had to watch my dog spinning with excitement at the prospect of a walk. Max was important to me for all sorts of reasons, but as I moved on from those lost years locked inside my own home, I recognised something that could still bring me to tears: his constant companionship, drive and spirit had given me this chance at a second life.

Before the accident, had anyone suggested I would be thriving in a new job that often saw me on call through the night, I would say they were mad. When my phone rang at three in the morning, however, I didn't surface from sleep with a sense of dread. It was exciting. A chance to get out and about on an adventure with Max as if we were the only two living souls. I loved it and the fact that Max adored it too just made the whole experience more rewarding. It could be a strange existence and sometimes I'd be ready for bed as dawn rose, but with careful management of my time, it worked out just fine.

When Max first moved in, I worried about Angela. She had never shared her home with any kind of pet and I knew from experience that a Springer Spaniel could charge indoors after a long and muddy walk before I had even got my boots off. Max was different, however. Sure, if there was a puddle he would rush to crash into it, but when it mattered, he listened to me. I talked to him constantly, which must have helped him tune in to my voice, but it served a useful purpose around my wife when it came to acclimatising her to a dog's life. He would wait in the van until I invited him to hop out and let me towel him down on the step before heading into the house. In return, Max had an uncanny ability to pick up on my thoughts and feelings. If I was tired or in pain on a walk, he would stay closer to me than usual, and when I needed him to thrash through a stately home after dark in full voice, he did so without hesitation. The connection between us was extraordinary and I wasn't alone in remarking upon it. Angela recognised what Max meant to me, as did friends and neighbours. Even people I had never met before were moved to comment on what a special relationship we shared. At the same time, as Max drew more likes and comments to my business page on Facebook, I decided it was time he had a profile of his own.

20

Max Out in the Lake District

BEFORE I BECAME A LOCKSMITH, shut away inside my house, I'd shown little interest in social media. I'd had a look at Facebook, but as far as I could see it was just a string of posts about the amazing lives that people led. It didn't seem to echo the real world. Everything was shiny and amazing, and nobody was posting the kind of updates I could identify with at the time. Instead of reading about cupcakes and running achievements, had I seen a post from someone that said they'd been tuned out in front of the television all day and felt like killing themselves, I could have identified with it. For this reason alone, I stayed away until I started the business.

My sole aim had been to drum up work. I could see that a Facebook page would be useful to raise my profile within the area. Everyone relied on locks in their everyday lives, even if they took that fact for granted. I just wanted to be the guy they called from the doorstep in a downpour and then raved about the speed and quality of my service in getting them into the dry. When I first took a picture of Max and shared it, I never imagined where it would take me. Without doubt, pictures of my dog helped to promote my work, but ultimately, I knew that people didn't flock to the page to remind themselves of my number.

Mindful of my first experience of Facebook, when it seemed that everyone was presenting an ideal image of themselves, I started a page dedicated to Max with a view to putting honesty at the heart of it. This was a dog who couldn't try to be anything but himself. He could be excitable and goofy, driven, dependable and constantly faithful. There was no pretence about Max, but he clearly lived life to the fullest and if that helped to bring some sunshine into someone's existence, rather than leaving them feeling like they had failed to measure up, then his page would serve a useful purpose.

'Shall we go live?' I asked Max on the evening that I finished setting up the community page. I had called it *Max Out in the Lake District* for two reasons. First, it did what it said on the tin, and second, it made me laugh. I wasn't trying to sell anything here and in many ways that took the pressure away. It was just fun. I had also splashed out on a digital camera because frankly, having Max had rekindled my love of photography. I began by uploading a recent picture of him and then sharing it on my locksmith page to make my followers aware. 'Congratulations,' I said as I finished tapping at the keyboard. Max regarded me from his basket. While I doubted he had any idea that he now had his own Facebook page, I knew he was content to see me relaxed and smiling. Leaving my computer, I spun around in my chair and dropped down to give him a cuddle. 'Don't be disappointed if it sinks without trace,' I said. 'But you never know, if one person stumbles across it and smiles, it'll be worthwhile.'

Over the weeks that followed, I aimed to post a picture every day. Sometimes, I'd switch to video mode and capture Max leaping in and out of the bracken and diving into water for a stick. I found a lot of my customers liked Max's page and somehow it felt liberating to be free from any obligation to promote my locksmith business. That was doing just fine through word of mouth and this was all about my dog. After work each evening, I'd visit the page and note the number of likes and comments was slowly building. People were also sharing my photographs and clips, and in turn that stoked further interest. I always moved aside so that Max could sniff the screen.

'See that?' I said to him and pointed out a comment from someone who said that they had turned one portrait of Max looking particularly serene into wallpaper for their phone. 'You're making a difference.'

A few weeks later, we set out on a lovely walk through a forest on a steep hillside overlooking the road into Keswick. We crossed a bridge over a plunging stream and followed a path carpeted in pine needles. Along the way, a young couple walking a Labrador took one look at Max and stopped me.

'Is this your dog?' the woman asked.

'It is.'

For a moment, I thought perhaps Max had been up to mischief in the brief moment he'd been out of my sight.

'Is it Max?' she asked, reaching down to pet him.

'That's right,' I said with some surprise and immediately assumed this was someone I should know. I wondered if she might be one of Angela's customers. I was often introduced to them by her as they came and went, and so now I just felt forgetful and rude.

'We love your photographs,' her partner said just then. 'My girlfriend here sends them to her mother.'

'She lives alone,' the woman said, rising to her feet now. 'You can't stop posting pictures now because she'll be on your case.'

'Consider me told,' I said, a little overwhelmed. 'And say hi to your mum from Max and me.'

The woman beamed and then exchanged a glance with her partner.

'Would Max mind posing for a photograph with me?' she asked. 'It would make Mum's day.'

'Be my guest,' I said and then invited the young man to hand me his camera phone so that they could both be in shot with him.

Of course, Max obliged quite happily and it was a joy to see them both grinning so broadly. They made a vague attempt to bring their Labrador into one more shot, but frankly, he was more interested in sniffing tree trunks. It was an encounter that lasted no more than a matter of minutes, but it would stay with me all day.

'Thank you so much,' said the young woman as we parted company. 'My mum won't believe it when we say that we've actually met Max.'

'It's our pleasure,' I said and wished them well on the rest of their walk.

As we turned to leave, she called out to me one more time.

'Mum is bound to ask me,' she said. 'What's your name?'

I have never been one to enjoy taking the stage. I like to be in the wings, offering my support from there. As time passed, and Max drew more attention both online and outdoors, I was content to be the guy in the background. Angela found it quite funny, especially when we went for our daily lunch in Portinscale. There, diners would venture meekly to our bench and enquire if this was indeed the Spaniel from the internet.

'And this is Kerry,' Angela would say, but by then Max would be at the centre of their attention.

I didn't mind one bit. In fact, I loved the fact that my dog could have such an impact. I kept having to remind myself that when I first met Max he was alone in a yard and just seeking a little company. We had given that to each other alright, but over time it had become clear to me that he was one of a kind. He wasn't particularly trained when I met him, nor did I set about teaching him many new tricks. Apart from his ability to mouse on command, and no doubt scaring the living daylights out of burglars across the Lake District, he just seemed to instinctively know how to click with me. One afternoon, after I had dropped Angela home and following a long job at a holiday home dismantling a particularly stubborn lock, we drove up to Latrigg. Clouds like Zeppelins had been cruising across the sky all afternoon, and as the sun set, I thought I might capture a nice picture of Max on the bench at the summit.

Sure enough, when we got there, the setting sun had turned the sky to glowing embers. I didn't have much time before it all faded.

'Max,' I said as we approached the bench overlooking Keswick and the majestic lake, 'show me how it's done.'

As I set up my camera, Max hopped up onto the bench. There, gazing out towards the darkening ridge beyond and the crimson crescent behind it, he settled on his haunches. The light on his coat was incredible, turning the tan patches to a deep russet, but when it came to taking photographs, it was always about his ears. All I had to do was find the most dramatic framing, call his name so he looked at me, and I had the perfect picture of my best friend in his element.

'That's lovely,' said Angela when I showed her the shots I had taken. 'Another one for Max's Facebook page?'

I had been gazing at each image when she joined me in the front room. Max lay in his bed beside my chair, snoring contentedly. Having reeled off quite a few frames, I just wanted to make sure I selected the best.

'Actually, this is for a competition,' I told her. 'I'm going to send a few, though I don't suppose I'll get anywhere. Still, you never know!'

Earlier that week, I had picked up a copy of BBC *Countryfile* magazine from the newsagent. As a lover of the outdoors, I always watched the TV show with enthusiasm. The magazine was a good read as well, and when I spotted the invitation to submit a favourite photograph that celebrated life outdoors, I knew I had to enter. I showed Angela the page in the magazine and then the photograph I was inspecting.

'There's a little bit of mud on his paw,' she noted, peering at the shot.

'You don't have to worry,' I said with a grin, knowing how meticulous Angela could be about cleanliness. 'I scrubbed him down before he came into the house.'

Angela turned her attention to the Spaniel out cold beside me. It had been another long and rewarding day. Max looked happily exhausted, which is exactly how I felt.

'One of my customers was asking after him earlier,' she said. 'She follows his Facebook page.'

'It's amazing how a little dog like Max could make such a big impression.'

As I said this, Angela wrinkled her nose.

'Oh, Kerry!' she said and wafted a hand across her face. At the same time, the smell reached my nostrils.

'Sorry,' I said on Max's behalf, 'he's just had his tea.'

21

The Great Flood

LATER THAT AUTUMN, dark clouds moved in over the fells and settled over Keswick. Summer had been hot and still, it seemed that it might never end. Then, just as Max and I were looking forward to cooler evening walks, the rain began.

At the time, the ground was so parched that it absorbed the water like a sponge. The cracks in the trail paths on our favourite walks soon swelled and sealed, however, and then the mud began to form. As we spent so much time outdoors, on the road and out in the countryside, I noticed the change very quickly and my heart sank a little. I don't mind bad conditions. In fact, I used to revel in them as a mountain biker, but this weather front was relentless. It poured from one day to the next, with just fleeting glimpses of the sun.

After a week, Max and I abandoned some of our favourite routes. While Max didn't seem to care one bit and positively enjoyed getting soaked, we'd both return to the van so caked in mud that it became a chore to clean ourselves up. Instead, we stuck to the shoreline paths around the

Lakes. It didn't stop Max from getting wet, of course, but I could at least just dry his towel afterwards rather than having to smuggle it into the washing machine when Angela wasn't looking.

A fortnight into the deluge, every brook and stream that once trickled down the hills had become pulsing arteries. Waterways appeared that I had never noticed before. It made it hard to ignore just how much rain had fallen for it all seemed to sweep down every incline.

Almost one month after the rain began, the storm clouds sheared apart and the sun shone through. By now, the ground underfoot was completely waterlogged. Whenever Max and I went off the path, my boots just sank into the slop. The earth was completely sodden, even high up on the hills. It would take a long time to dry out.

It was strange to see people emerge from houses and shops without snapping open an umbrella or hurrying for cars or shelter. The sun glistened from puddles in the streets and water gurgled through the gutters and drains. Whenever I passed the river that ran through town, swollen and fast-moving as it carried the runoff from the fells to the lake, I was struck by what a lucky escape we'd had. In the past, some properties had suffered a little flooding during heavy rains. In fact, I found a new branch of my business became quite popular as the river level rose. I'd come across domestic flood barriers that could be installed across doorways and it seemed to tie in nicely with my line of work. When the rain started, I found myself fitting quite a few units along riverfront properties as well as holiday lets in low-lying pockets of the region. It kept me busy, but I was grateful when the good weather returned because it just made our walks more pleasant.

One week after the rains, Max and I had taken off south towards Borrowdale. There, we'd gone for a ramble along the ridge overlooking Derwentwater. From there, judging by the way the islands looked squeezed, it seemed to me that the lake was at full capacity. It was a blustery, unsettled morning, but we weren't going to let it spoil our chance of fresh air. It was only when I noted that the clouds clawing in were beginning to darken and knot together that I realised we were in for more rain.

'Let's hope it's just a shower, eh?' I said to Max as he bounded back to show me his stick. 'Light drizzle is about all we can handle.'

In the van, on our way to the next job, I switched the wipers on intermittent. Within minutes, however, I had pushed the lever and they were sweeping back and forth at full pelt. I slowed down as the downpour picked up and glanced nervously at Max.

'We might have some problems in town,' I said, raising my voice above the sound of hammering rain. 'If the lake is full, there's nowhere for the runoff to go.'

By the time we got home, the rain was torrential. There was just no end to it. On the drive down to Keswick, the standing water on the road had caused the traffic to back up. Even the drains on our street were struggling to cope with the volume. When Angela finished work and joined us in the front room, she found me looking anxiously from the window.

'It's going to flood,' I said to her. 'I'm sure of it.'

'Do you have to be on call tonight?' she asked me. 'Wouldn't it be better to stay indoors?'

'If anyone needs me then I should go,' I said and then turned my attention to the dog on his bed to remind her that I wasn't alone. 'Wherever I go, Max will be at my side.'

Given the number of properties that had appointed me keyholder, it was no surprise when I received a phone call in the early hours. According to the handler at the response centre, the fire brigade had attended reports of a flooding at a remote and empty manor on my watch and they required access to a particular wing. The address was over near Ullswater, which was a 10- to 12-minute drive away.

'We'll be back in no time,' I promised Angela when she stirred as I crept out of bed.

It was almost an hour before Max and I pulled up beside the fire engine outside the manor. The drive had been dreadful, with roads blocked by water at almost every turn.

'We weren't sure you would make it,' said the officer in charge as we made our way inside the building. Max followed dutifully behind, which drew the man's attention. 'Your dog doesn't seem bothered by the drama.'

'He's my head of security,' I explained. 'It's all in a night's work for him.'

With the two big oak doors to the wing unlocked, I returned to the van with Max and let the fire brigade do their job. A couple of the guys remained with the engine. They told me they had been run off their feet since their shift began, with call-outs like this one coming in from across the region.

'Where are you heading now?' one asked me.

'Keswick,' I said.

The two guys glanced at one another.

'Be careful,' one said as Max jumped into the van.

It had been bad on the journey out. On our return, the sheer volume of water coming off the hillsides had turned to a crescendo. Half a mile down the lane, we came across a torrent coming straight over a wall. I pulled up, with the beams on full, and stepped out with Max just to see for myself how bad it really was. The lane here dipped before sinking around to the right. All I could see was a foaming rapid barrelling high up the outer wall.

'We're not risking that,' I told Max, who was equally gripped by the spectacle in front of us. 'I know you love to swim, but this is different.'

Having turned the van around, and followed the high road towards town, it struck me how serious things had become. Max and I were totally alone, there was no other traffic. The night sky looked more like the deep-sea depths, with water crashing over the windscreen and leaves tumbling wildly. This wasn't a game, it was a matter of life or death. I checked that Max was properly strapped in and carefully negotiated yet another stretch of water that spanned the road.

The flooding was widespread and with Keswick in a basin I worried about what I might find. I knew that Angela would be safe, for our street was some distance from the river. Even so, it ran through the heart of town and then crossed under a bridge before broadening out to feed the lake. Many hundreds of homes would be at risk, which made me feel quite sick.

'Let's see what we can do to help, Max,' I said, as we began our descent into town.

By now, we were following the water course. It skittered down the road in front of us, with only one destination. What should have been a short journey took me upwards of an hour. Around three in the morning, I popped home to check on Angela and found her waiting for me.

'Thank goodness,' she said as Max and I came in through the door.

'I'm just here for my waterproofs,' I said. 'I've got a bunch of door flood barriers in the back of the van. If I can help anyone, I need to get to work fast.'

'Will you be taking Max?' she asked as he slinked around her feet for a drink from his bowl.

I had just grabbed my wellingtons from under the coat rack and turned to see my wife looking deeply anxious.

'As long as Max is with me, everything will always be fine,' I promised her.

Moving at a crawl through the floods, we made our way towards the bottom end of town. Some of the roads looked more like channels, with water lapping over the kerbs. We passed some residents who were barricading their paths. I pulled up on the pavement at the corner and for the next few hours set about fitting all the damns I had in the back to any property that looked at serious risk if the river breached her banks. By dawn, mindful that Max had been so good sitting in the van, I headed across to the park so he could stretch his legs. The river forms a boundary on one side. It was a truly frightening sight to see and to hear the volume of water surging towards the bridge that carried the main road around the lake. Keswick had suffered flooding in the past and so the authorities had installed tall barriers to protect the road. Looking at the powerful rapids now, however, I wasn't convinced it would be sufficient. It was still pouring with rain and much of the runoff from the mountains would take a little while to reach this level.

'Max,' I said as he trotted alongside me, 'we still have work to do.'

For the rest of the morning, I worked alongside the residents of Keswick to prepare for the inevitable. Together with friends and neighbours, and people I had seen around town but never spoken to before, I helped haul furniture up stairs and drop sandbags in place. Throughout, we kept one eye on the river. There was no longer a drop down the bank to the water level. It snaked alongside the park in a quite malevolent manner and the police were wise to lock off the path alongside it. Max remained in the van so I could focus on helping out. With the window open, he proved a popular draw for children and a good distraction as their parents worked tirelessly to protect property from the incoming flood. Every now and then I'd return to the van and let him out. Max would find himself surrounded by curious children and bathed in the attention.

'What a star,' one mother said. 'He's very calm, isn't he?'

'Let's hope we can all be like Max,' I said warily, casting my eye towards the river.

At lunchtime, Max and I returned home for something to eat. I was exhausted, but a looming sense of dread had seized the town: we knew the flood was coming, the question was when. An hour later, I drove out with Max to see what else could be done. This time, on heading down to the lakeside road, I found the police had closed the bridge. The barriers designed to prevent flooding could do nothing to contain the sheer body of water. Blue lights blinked on the tops of fire trucks and squad cars, while people sploshed to and fro, looking like they'd scrambled from their houses in a hurry. For a while, in shock like everyone else, I stood with Max and watched the flood pooling across the approach to the bridge. Within half an hour, the police were forced to pull the cordon even further back. Then, with tarmac disappearing under water, they closed the entire road.

By now, with the riverbanks breached, safety was the number one priority for everyone. Some of the roads alongside the river had become torrents. With manhole covers blown from the drains, you couldn't just wade along without serious risk of drowning. The water was also choked with debris and potentially lethal where it swept and churned along. It didn't stop us all from coming together to help each other and save what we could. As the water from the mountains reached the town, the flooding proved both merciless and relentless. It also continued through the night.

Over the course of the next three days, I lent a hand wherever we could but it was Max who proved a lifeline. While I went into houses to help people salvage their belongings, he would stay outside with family members who were too young, frail or distraught to assist. As conditions became seriously hazardous, I'd fitted him with a bright red canine jacket. It made him look like part of the emergency services and in a way he provided a vital service. He would pad towards anyone in distress and just stand close beside them. Often, he'd prove to be just the distraction they needed. Sometimes I would come out to find somebody crouching beside him, giving him a cuddle, ruffling his long ears or drying their eyes on his coat. Max would simply stand there, giving them all the time they needed. As a source of comfort, he was basically offering people what he had given to me. It made me so proud of him.

In the days that followed, as the water began to subside, Keswick emerged as a community in grief. Over 300 properties had been flooded out. People had lost so much and Max was there for every one of them. Even the electric guys who were working tirelessly to restore power thought he was fantastic. He'd go and sit by them as they worked on junction boxes and they would make a fuss of him. With journalists roaming in search of stories from the drama, he even got a mention in the local paper. It was a testing time in the history of my home town, yet one dog with a calm manner and gentle soul had reminded everyone that no matter how bleak things seem, there is always hope.

22

Reaching Out

'WHY HAVE YOU CHOSEN a new van with three front seats?'

This was Angela's first response when Max and I pulled up outside the house in our new mobile office. Business was shaping up nicely and I felt it was time to upgrade our vehicle.

'Simple,' I said, as she peered inside while Max sniffed around behind me. 'I didn't think it would be fair to make you sit in the back.'

My wife laughed and rolled her eyes. She knew that everywhere I went, Max rode alongside me. In the old van, if we were heading out for lunch, Angela would inspect the passenger seat and complain if she found a dog hair. Even if I had brushed it in advance, however, once she climbed in, Max would inevitably bundle in after her and spark an outburst of shrieking. In choosing a replacement for my old van, I wanted to make sure there was room for us all.

On driving out of Keswick, on our way to lunch, I felt blessed to be in the company of my loving wife and loyal dog. Naturally, Max chose the window seat. He's one of those dogs who likes to feel the rush of air against his muzzle, while Angela simply wanted to travel without a Spaniel on her lap while we caught up with each other. With a new career that was getting bigger and better, and a sense that Max had something to offer the wider word, I felt happy and fulfilled. It was a far cry from the man I had been and the lonely child locked away inside his head, who just wanted to be loved.

Over lunch, with Max at my feet, I switched my phone to silent so that Angela and I could talk. Naturally, Max drew his admirers. Neither of us minded when people came up and asked if it was the dog from Facebook. It was lovely, in fact, especially if anyone told us their story about what Max meant to them.

'Excuse me, would you mind if my mother met your dog?

We were just finishing our coffee when a teenage girl approached with her request and then apologised for interrupting. She was very shy but ever so sweet, and both Angela and I were at pains to say it was no trouble at all. The girl brought her mother across, who greeted Max like an old friend. In conversation, we learned that she was recovering from a serious illness. Keeping up with Max's escapades across the Lake District had been a source of delight for her and also motivation, she said.

'We thought we'd follow Max's example and get out of the house,' her daughter told me. 'This is Mum's first outing in a long time.'

'Congratulations,' I said.

'We should be thanking you,' she replied and tickled Max behind the ears. 'Seeing your photographs every day made me realise how much I needed to get outdoors.'

It was moments like this, as well as the steady stream of messages and comments on Max's Facebook feed, that I found so touching. Angela was just as moved by the encounter. She had seen how Max had transformed my life and given me hope. Now, here he was having the very same impact on other people experiencing personal challenges and obstacles. We left the cafe on a high that afternoon. Having belted Max in once Angela had taken the middle seat, I turned my phone off mute and checked to see if I had any messages. I read a text from a wholesaler to confirm a part I had been waiting for was now in stock and then switched to my email.

Then, having read the only one that had arrived while we were at lunch, I climbed into the driver's seat and looked at Angela in disbelief.

'Remember the photographs I sent in to the *Countryfile* competition?'

'I liked those,' said Angela. 'What about them?'

I turned the key in the ignition, still facing my wife.

'We won!'

She looked surprised and delighted.

'Amazing! Which picture?'

'You're not going to believe this,' I said. 'We came first, second, third … and fourth!'

It was such a thrill to see Max in my favourite magazine. I was on a high about it for a long time. Customers went out and bought copies, and of course word spread when I shared it on Facebook. Max's page was growing in popularity every day and of course I had to keep it fresh. In looking for new and interesting photoshoot locations in between jobs, we would regularly venture off the beaten track and make new discoveries in a region that I loved.

One windswept day, Max and I took a walk that we had done countless times before along the lake. It's a beautiful place to be, with a majestic body of water contained by rugged, forested slopes, but nothing out of the ordinary for us. I had taken so many photographs of him around the shoreline that I had lost count.

On this particular outing, however, great gusts of wind were scouring the lake and kicking up waves against the rocky outcrops. It was quite something to see. In fact, Max paid particular attention because there is a bench near one crag that he liked to run up to and sit on while waiting for me. I had my phone that day and thought it would be good to see if I could capture a picture of the water as it crashed against the rocks. I drew closer to Max, thinking about where to position myself so I could capture the water spreading wide on impact, and that's when I noticed his ears. In the wind, they were flapping and snapping ten to the dozen.

'Stay right where you are,' I told him and switched my phone from camera to video.

It was only a short clip, but it made me laugh. Back home, I uploaded it to Facebook and jokingly suggested Max could rank the wind strength by his 'flap-o-meters'.

That evening, activity on my dog's page went berserk. Every time I looked, the clip had received thousands of new hits.

'This is unbelievable,' I said to Angela when I showed her. 'Who'd have thought a pair of Spaniel ears would have this effect?'

'Well, you saw something in them,' she said. 'With so much bad news floating around the world, this kind of thing puts a smile on people's faces.'

'It's hardly Hollywood quality, though.'

'That's all part of the charm.' Angela handed me back my phone. 'It's simple and quite clear from every post you share that you and Max adore each other.'

Twenty-four hours after I had noticed Max's ears trying to take off, the video clip had earned one million views. It was hard to believe, but a fun experience. At the time, about 4,000 additional people had liked his page so they would receive updates on their feed as I posted them. Every time I looked at my phone, that number had climbed even higher. The next day at lunch, I broke my own rule and kept my phone on the table so I could keep an eye on the numbers.

'At this rate,' I said to Angela, 'Max will have 10,000 fans by Christmas.'

A few weeks later, on Christmas Eve, we hit the number I had predicted. With such a huge upswing in the community surrounding Max came further interest in his story. What was it about this Springer Spaniel, people wanted to know, that had such a calming and restorative effect? I couldn't provide any clear answer, but it was something I dwelled on over that festive period. In some ways, I suppose a calm, loyal and stoic dog like Max could be all things to all people and that was fine by me. He was the lifeline I'd been seeking as a castaway in my own home. To others, he embodied hope or inspiration, even just a reminder at a time of loneliness that you always had a four-legged friend.

It started me thinking that with the right support, perhaps Max could help more people.

Which is where he began his journey to becoming a therapy dog.

'The purpose of this assessment,' the lady from the charity said, having met me in the park as arranged one day, 'is to test how Max reacts in the face of different behaviours. It's vital a therapy dog can handle anything.'

'Understood,' I said, and quietly hoped Max wouldn't spot a squirrel at that moment in time. 'He's super cool.'

Therapy Dogs Nationwide do incredible work with people in need of canine comfort, distraction or just a shared moment that brightens their day. I knew Max had the temperament – I just hoped the charity representative would see those qualities that marked him out to me. Turning to Max now, who sat obediently beside me, the charity representative invited him to hop up onto the picnic table. Max obliged her and then immediately lay down when she asked him. I stood back, feeling tense but so proud of my boy. Next, she poked and prodded him. Max looked at me as if to say, 'Did you put her up to this?' but remained quite chilled. He barely blinked when she slapped the table beside him and again with a book she took from her bag. Then she switched from trying to startle him to effectively smothering him with love. She stroked, hugged and tickled him, and naturally, Max just absorbed whatever she directed at him.

I knew he had passed even before I received confirmation by letter a week later. My Moo had just been such a natural with her. All I could do was beam with pride at him. As I saw things, it was another stage on our journey together. With his fame growing, through Facebook and his star turn in *Countryfile* magazine, I felt that I had found a way to channel it into a force for good. As much as I adored my career alongside my loyal head of security, and the adventures we took on in between jobs, it meant our days became even busier. I had his red coat emblazoned with SUPPORT DOG in accordance with the charity's standards and took on visits to retirement homes, hospices and anyone who would benefit from a shared moment with my Max.

Along with his growing profile, Max began to receive more interest from the media. As I mentioned earlier, he'd featured in a local newspaper for his comforting presence during the flood, and of course his photographs in *Countryfile* magazine had added to his legion of admirers. The Flapometer clip continued to draw visits to his page from all over the world and I began to hear him described as 'an internet sensation'. This made me chuckle whenever we settled down with Angela at the end of the day. If the fire was on, Max would lie there gently snoring or blowing off, and I would think, 'Yup, what a pin-up!' In reality, I was so thrilled for him and also quite happy to be known as 'the owner'. I had no desire for the spotlight to fall on me.

Then everything changed with a phone call.

A journalist from a regional lifestyle magazine had been keeping up with Max's Facebook escapades and wanted to profile him. Thinking this would help spread the word about his work as a therapy dog, I agreed without hesitation. I figured she would make a big fuss of Max, he'd pose for a photo and I could look forward to visiting my newsagent to see if I could spot him.

'Kerry, if I may, let's talk about you,' she said when we met, which took me aback. 'You say that Max helped you through a dark time. Perhaps you could go into more detail for me?'

In telling people the story about how Max had come into my life, I had been careful to filter the more personal aspects. I wasn't comfortable sharing the fact that I had suffered depression as a result of my chronic pain and considered taking my own life. I didn't want anyone to know I had become so fearful of the outside world that I lived like a hermit. I worried people would think I was off my rocker. As a younger man, if someone was classed as having a mental-health issue, you'd mark them down as a nutter to be avoided. Things were very different in those days, but I still felt as if there was a stigma attached to it. So, instead, I just went with the angle that I'd met Max when things weren't going too well for me, took some photographs of him up on the fells and he'd become a big deal on Facebook. The journalist was sitting beside me on the sofa. She had a little voice recorder rolling and a note-pad on her lap. She'd nodded her way through everything I'd had to tell her up to this point and now here she was, waiting for me to tell her the whole story.

'There's not much to say,' I told her awkwardly. 'I'd been in a traffic accident and it took me a while to get back on my feet.'

'In what way?' she asked. 'In your own words, Kerry.'

I looked at Max. A sense of panic rose inside me, but I held it back. I told myself that he never complained when I asked him to pose for a photograph, or stand quietly while children crowded around him. If he could do this to help people, I thought just then, perhaps I could do the same by sharing my story.

'Okay ...' I cleared my throat, took a moment to find my voice and took her back to a time of my life I had tried to shut down.

I felt awful afterwards. I really wasn't sure I had done the right thing and fretted about it for days on end. As I'd taken the journalist through the bleakest moments in my story, I found myself skirting around a word until I just swallowed hard and voiced it: depression. I had suffered from it throughout that time, but it had only really been since finding strength through Max that I was able to face up to it. Even so, it felt like I had released a genie from a bottle. Angela was lovely about it and provided nothing but reassurance. At the same time, Max came into his own: he just knew that I was fretting. Whether I was walking, parked in the van and staring through the windscreen or nursing a cup of tea at the kitchen table, I would feel a muzzle brush me, look down and find him looking at me as if to say everything would be alright.

On the day of publication, I picked up the magazine with trembling hands. Sure enough, there was the article and the story I had shared about my depression. The journalist had done a responsible job with it, yet I felt so exposed. I told myself that hopefully not many people I knew would see it and tried to put it to the back of my mind.

That day, the first messages began to appear in Max's Facebook feed. I dreaded seeing the notification icon, which was something I had grown to love, but then I read what people were saying. In every case, they were surprised I hadn't been more transparent about what I'd been through, but congratulated me on the courage I'd shown in opening up. They said it now made sense why Max meant so much to me and offered nothing but support, love and encouragement. Their reaction moved me to tears, which wasn't difficult, but I felt like we were at the heart of such an outpouring of affection.

At the same time, as the messages continued to roll in, many people began to share their stories of struggles with their own mental health. What I'd started as a little place to celebrate my Springer Spaniel had become a community for those seeking respite from challenging times in their lives. Whether seeing a picture of Max messing about in the countryside cheered them up over a cup of coffee or encouraged them to feel they too could regain control over their lives, his Facebook page brought sunshine and hope to many people.

Now my story was out there, too. I had thought it would be a difficult and regrettable experience. Instead, people kept on coming forward to thank me for being so open and sharing their own experience of depression. It did me the power of good to feel that humans could come together like this, with a dog as the unifying force. I didn't feel at all embarrassed. In fact, it came as a liberation.

23

And Then There was Paddy ...

I TAKE A GREAT DEAL OF CARE over Max's teeth. They weren't in great condition when I first met him and so over the years I have ferried him to the vet on a regular basis to have them checked over. One time, in 2017, the vet decided that Max would benefit from a deep clean. This involved putting him under with an anaesthetic and then giving him a scrape and polish so his teeth sparkled. It was a routine procedure. All I had to do was drop him off at the practice, go to work for the day and pick him up on the way home.

The staff know that I can be emotional when it comes to Max and his welfare. There has been many a time when I've wiped away a tear while buying something as mundane as flea treatment. I'm a mess, and very happy to laugh at myself about it.

'How will you manage?' one nurse joked with me as I handed Max into their care.

'Just take good care of him,' I said with a chuckle. 'I'm looking forward to seeing his million-dollar smile!'

It was a light-hearted exchange, but as I left, it felt as if a dead weight had attached itself to my shoulders. I climbed back in the van, mindful that I had a work appointment to keep, and then simply froze.

Beside me, Max's seat was empty.

It was the first time I had been in the van without him and it left me feeling bereft. I had one hand on the ignition key at the time, ready to twist the engine into life. Instead, I let go, took a sharp, involuntary breath and wept.

I got it together within a few minutes, yet it left me painfully aware that one day Max would no longer be here. We had been friends for such a long time. While we were both getting on in age, he was no longer the young dog I had first met. There was plenty of life left in him, of course, but the realisation hit me hard. Immediately, it dredged up memories of how I had felt when Zak passed away without warning. I was bereft then and didn't want to go back to feeling that way ever again. What's more, Max had saved me from an existence so dark, I could see no light. Somehow, I panicked that if he left me now I would return to that place. I just wasn't confident I could cope without him and that shook me to the core.

Throughout work all day, I checked my phone awaiting a message or a call from the surgery. I wanted to know that Max was okay, yet I dreaded hearing the ringtone or a chime to say I had a text in case something had gone wrong. When the vet finally contacted me to say that Max was up and running, and enjoying lots of cuddles from the team, I dropped everything to collect him.

Looking back, I knew I had just got into a panic. Even so, it made me painfully aware that I would never cope without another dog like Max. That started me wondering whether he would enjoy another canine companion. It would give him a friend to play with and teach how to jump from the jetty, and help me to continue enjoying the confidence and sense of happiness that Max had brought me.

Without question, if I was to invite another dog into our lives, it had to be a Springer Spaniel. I just loved the intensity of the bond I had with Max. It was one I had shared with Zak through his short life, and I saw it in other Springers and their owners. This was a dog who thrived on human companionship, and led by example when it came to celebrating life. With this in mind, I began to look online for breeders in the area. It became a quiet bedtime routine of mine, though I did so with my screen angled away from Angela and her book.

'What are you so interested in?' she'd ask sometimes.

'Oh, nothing,' I'd say, having quickly switched to a parts supplier website. 'The usual.'

In a way, it was a little pipe dream. I'd gone to great lengths to persuade Angela to let me take on Max. Admittedly, she knew that my life effectively depended on it, but I didn't think I could argue the same case again. I was also aware that she had made great concessions by allowing Max to join us. She'd become really fond of him, of course, and wouldn't want it any other way, but he was my dog, and responsibility for everything about him fell to me.

So, instead of discussing it with her, I just fed my little fantasy by scouring breeder pages in search of a dog like Max. I even focused my search around Carlisle, because I vaguely remembered Max's former owner telling me he had come from somewhere up there. It was a pipe dream, and went against sensible advice about trying to replicate a beloved dog. The more I looked, however, the more I convinced myself it had to be done. Impulsively, perhaps, but in a bid to fill a deep-seated fear that I would not be able to cope without a dog, I was driven to finding a Springer as quiet and calm as Max.

And then I got Paddy.

When I found the advert for the litter, I knew my search was over. I vaguely recognised the name of the breeder as a friend of a friend. She was also based close to Carlisle, which was good enough for me. This was on a Friday evening. I popped out to the van, pretending to collect some bits, and called the number from there. It went to answering machine. I left a message, and again an hour later. On phoning one more time, and recording one more message in case they'd missed the last two, I finished with a grimace and a rather low opinion of myself.

'What am I like?' I asked Max, who had crept out of the house with me.

The next day, I was due to drive Angela to Penrith, so she could catch a train to London for a weekend with friends. On the way to the station, with Max riding alongside her, I kept drawing breath to ask how she'd feel about two dogs in the passenger seat. Every time, however, my confidence deserted me and I'd simply ask about her plans.

By the time I waved her goodbye, I turned and cursed myself for being so spineless. Rejoining Max in the van, I decided to drive home and forget all about it. With no response from the breeder, and being too cowardly to even raise the subject with my own wife, I decided this was where reality dawned.

'Never mind, eh?' I said. 'Let's drive somewhere nice and go for a walk.'

I hadn't even turned out of the station car park before the phone rang. I recognised the number straight away – I had called it enough times, after all. Immediately, I assumed the breeder was calling to ask me to delete her number and stop bothering her.

'Hello?' I said awkwardly, having pulled back into a parking bay to take the call. 'Yes, that's right. I have left a few messages ... I was wondering if I could take a look at the litter.' My voice trailed away there as my confidence deserted me. Then, having answered a series of searching questions about my experience with dogs, my expression turned from dread to delight when she asked if I could go round at one o'clock.

We had plenty of time, yet I drove like the clappers. In fact, at midday we were parked up outside the entrance to the farm she had given me as her address. I didn't want to look like a stalker, so I took Max for a walk up and down the lane a couple of times. Over the phone, she had said that someone else was coming to view the puppies before me. On every pass, I felt sure that whoever it was would be there to take the last one available. Finally, towards our appointed visiting time, I came around to see that one of the cars outside the farmhouse had gone. Popping Max in the van, I pulled into the vacated space and knocked on the door as if I had just arrived.

The lady who answered the door was warm and charming. Inside, before viewing the puppies, I told her I already had a Springer and just wanted to see if any would fit his nature. She looked at me quizzically.

'You look familiar,' she said. 'From Facebook?'

'Possibly,' I said bashfully, and told her I ran a page for my dog, who was waiting for me in the van outside.'

'It's not Max, is it?' she asked and when I said it was, she insisted I bring him in to meet her.

It was the perfect icebreaker before she introduced me to a gorgeous litter of pups in her front room. They were only four weeks old, with another month to go before they could move on to their new homes. Even so, I knew I had to pick one and it needed to be a boy like Max. They say you don't choose a puppy, a puppy chooses you. In this case, I picked up one scamp with a hind leg that was completely brown. I held him up to my face just to say hello, but before I could draw breath, he licked my nose.

That was it.

I was smitten.

'We'll have this one,' I said, and crouched to show Max his new canine apprentice.

With the deposit paid, I drove home wondering how on earth I was going to sell this to Angela. I asked Max out loud, but he wasn't much help. So, once I got home, I decided the surest way to ease the stress I had put myself under was to make that all-important call.

'Ange,' I said once she'd told me about her journey, 'there's something I need to ask. You know, recently I was worried about how I'd manage if I ever lost Max? Well, I've been thinking about a way forward.'

'We're not getting another dog,' she said frankly. 'Kerry, I couldn't cope with two.'

At once, my heart sank. I looked down at Max, who seemed equally crestfallen. It was then, in a blink, I realised I had just one chance at this.

'It's fair to say I'm cheap to keep, right?'

'I suppose,' she said with some hesitation, as if unsure where this was going.

'I don't drink, I don't smoke, I don't go to the pub with the lads and watch football, or expect a roast on a Sunday.'

'Thank goodness!'

'I don't ask for anything, but just this once, I'm asking you to let me get another dog. It's all I want, but I need your blessing.'

In response, my wife sighed down the line.

'It's not a big dog, is it?'

'No,' I said, and then cleared my throat. 'Not really.'

'And it won't make a mess?'

'Of course not!'

'Or chew anything?' she added.

'Out of the question. Please, Ange, I'll take full responsibility. Just do this for me.'

'I'm not sure,' she said after a moment.

'I'll buy you a Mulberry handbag,' I said in desperation. 'Whatever you want!'

This time she laughed.

'Oh, go on then! You can spend the weekend looking for breeders.'

'I've already done that,' I confessed. 'He's coming in four weeks.'

A fortnight later, I took Max back to the breeder's home so he could properly meet the puppy. We introduced them in the garden. I recorded a video of the encounter and uploaded it to Max's Facebook page. It blew up overnight. The next day, Radio Cumbria rang and asked me what he was called.

'I haven't decided yet,' I said, having been overwhelmed by suggestions from fans of the page, 'but I can tell you by the end of the week.'

'Please do,' said the man from the station. 'We'll put it out on the news bulletin.'

It was an exciting time and the public interest also made it a little bit crazy. All of a sudden, having promised to come up with a name, I struggled to think of anything suitable. One evening that week, I was flicking through the channels and found myself engrossed in a *Star Wars* film. I have always liked them. It's great escapism, and in a way that's what Max offered me. I dwelled on it for a while in front of the film and the next day I rang the station.

'In the *Star Wars* universe, an apprentice Jedi is called a Padawan,' I explained. 'As the new pup will be guided by Max, we're calling him Paddy Padawan.'

Twenty-four hours later, following the news broadcast, everyone in the region knew the name of the new pup before he'd even left the litter.

* * *

Naturally, the night before the big day, I could not sleep a wink. I'd already bought a little travel bed that fitted to a seat belt and placed that on the bench beside Max so that he could watch over him. Max joined me on the drive out to collect him. My heart was thumping the whole way there. I wanted to pick up Paddy early to give me the day to settle him in. The handover felt like a dream, and was made so much easier by the fact that the breeder told me how much she was looking forward to keeping up with Paddy's progress via the Facebook page. She was understandably attached to her pups, having raised such a fit and healthy litter. It was lovely to think she could check in on him like this.

'I'll be posting photographs,' I promised her. 'Just you try and stop me!'

Back home, as Paddy explored the ground floor of his new home, Angela looked on warily. 'Why do I sense trouble?' she asked as he sniffed around under Max's watchful eye.

'Relax,' I said. 'Let's take him out to lunch with us. The sooner he gets into our routine, you won't even know he's there.'

I hadn't considered the fact that with four of us in the front of the vehicle, Paddy would have to sit on Angela's lap. As we set off, I watched her clasp him tenderly and hoped it might be a bonding experience.

'He is sweet,' she said, a little reluctantly, as we approached the long winding lane that took us to the cafe.

A few minutes later, just before we drove through the gates, Paddy was sick all over her.

'Get him off me!' she shrieked and rushed to the toilets to clean herself up.

Fortunately, for all the fuss, my wife could see already what Paddy meant to me. We enjoyed a good lunch with the pup in my care this time, but on dropping Angela home, I decided not to leave Paddy there for a nap.

'He can come to work with me,' I said. 'He has a little bed to rest in and Max will take good care of him.'

'Are you sure?' she said.

'I've never been more certain,' I told her, and from that moment on, Paddy joined Max and me wherever we went.

Unlike Max, when I left Paddy in my office on the first night he kicked off like a howling banshee. I'd settled him in a pup crate, which offered him plenty of space but kept him safe. In the early hours I crumbled, popped down to the office to let him out, and he promptly fell asleep on my knee. I felt sorry for the poor little mite – he'd just left the comfort of his mum, brothers and sisters, and now here he was in a strange house with a massive dog trying to sleep in the same room as him. Eventually, I managed to return him to his crate, but I didn't get much shut-eye. Nor did Max, who seemed quite tired the next day.

The following evening, I was determined to be strong and resist the temptation to comfort Paddy. The quicker he settled, the sooner we could all enjoy some peace and quiet. So this time I left the door ajar on his crate, crept out of the office and then sighed to myself as the crying began. I pulled the door ajar, but stayed in the hallway. If it carried on, I thought to myself, I would have to separate the dogs so that at least Max got some rest. The mewling and howling carried on for a few minutes and then suddenly fell quiet. I peeped around the corner, saw Paddy flopping out of his crate and then tottering across the floor towards Max. There, he clambered into his basket and snuggled up against Max's belly. Aware of my presence, Max looked at me like I owed him big time. Then, with a sigh, he rested his chin on the little guy, enveloping him protectively.

24

Meet and Greet

'PADDY, LEAVE MAX ALONE! Stop swinging from his ear, he's not a playground.'

It's fair to say that the new puppy was hard to ignore. As ever, Max was a trooper in the face of relentless interest and mischief-making from young Paddy. I'd hear a yelp from the office, walk in and find him dangling from Max, which was probably great fun for Paddy but not so much for my old friend.

Having set out to find a Springer Spaniel puppy that was a carbon copy of Max, it became increasingly clear that Paddy could not have been more different. He shared many good points, being attentive and smart, loving, dependable and a pleasure to have around. It's just where Max could choose to shift through the gears depending on what we were doing, Paddy only had one speed and that was 100 miles per hour. Despite the difference in horsepower, Max handled him brilliantly. In no time, they became very close.

Introducing Paddy to the Facebook page was great fun. As he grew bigger and stronger, I found myself facing new challenges in capturing them both in photographs and short video clips. I loved it, as did both dogs, because it meant more time messing about up on the hills and trails.

As well as the likes, comments and messages from those who took pleasure in watching the adventures of two fun-loving Springer Spaniels, sometimes I received requests from people who wanted to meet the dogs in person. Often it was from dog-walkers in the region, but then Keswick attracts a lot of tourists. It's also a very dog-friendly town. So, a visitor who also happened to be a fan of the Facebook page might drop me a line to say they were staying for a week and wondered if it might be possible to meet Max and Paddy.

When the requests first began, I was always happy to arrange a time and place as long as I felt comfortable. It was rarely individuals and often families or elderly couples. If I clicked on their profile, then nine times out of ten there would be a Spaniel in the pictures they posted. It meant I enjoyed a pleasant walk with people who shared my interests and sometimes Max and Paddy would make a four-legged friend.

Over time, however, the appeal of my two buddies never failed to take me by surprise.

One day, I picked up a Facebook message from a lady in America. This wasn't unusual; people got in touch from all over the world. It was very short and to the point, and I was able to answer it very easily. The lady had seen the now-famous picture of Max on the bench at the top of Latrigg and wanted to know where it was.

Keswick, I wrote back to her.

Where is Keswick?

In the Lake District, I replied patiently.

A few minutes later, I received another message from her.

Where is the Lake District?

Aware that I needed to be a little more generous with my detail, I wrote a nice note back explaining that it was a beautiful region in the northwest of England and thought no more about it.

A fortnight passed before I received another message.

I'm coming over for a tour of the Lake District. Can I meet Max?

Naturally, by now, some alarm bells were ringing in my head. While I had never turned anyone down who wanted to spend time with us, I was always careful. This just seemed a bit intense, and yet when I had a look at her profile she seemed like an honest, quite delightful retiree with a passion for travel. At the same time, something told me nobody would seriously cross the Atlantic just to meet Max and so I sent a message back to humour her by suggesting she get in touch when she began her tour.

The next time I heard from her, I realised I had underestimated her commitment.

I've just landed in the UK. Will be in Keswick at 2pm on Wednesday. Are you and the dogs free to meet me then?

I was in the van when I read her message. Max and Paddy were on the bench beside me.

'What have I let myself in for?' I said aloud. 'You'll protect me, won't you?'

Paddy and Max both looked at me as if to suggest I should be doing that for them.

*   *   *

Come midweek, we were bathed in beautiful sunshine. Max and Paddy couldn't wait for me to finish a job and take them for a walk. They had no idea what I had in store for them. Worryingly, neither did I.

I had arranged to meet my new American friend at a popular tourist spot up on the fells. A lot of minibuses take visitors up there and the parking area seemed like a suitable meeting place. Crucially, it was in public view. So, if this sweet retiree turned out to be anything but that, I wasn't putting myself or the dogs in any danger.

There were no other vehicles at the meeting point when we arrived. I let Max and Paddy out for a play and then nervously kept one eye on the approach road. I had the keys to the van in my hand. Several times, I had to resist the temptation to jump back in, summon the dogs and drive away. When I heard the sound of a minibus grinding through the gears, just moments before it cleared the brow, I called Max to my side. Paddy was off chasing butterflies. I decided it might be best just to have my main man in the firing line.

'Stay cool,' I said to him, as much as to myself.

The tour bus pulled up on the other side of the car park. I watched the door open before a troop of tourists made their way down the steps. One in particular zoned in on me. I smiled as she crossed towards us.

'This must be Max,' she said in rich midwestern accent.

'It is indeed,' I said and stopped there because she was straight in without further word.

Max was brilliant, but then he's a natural when anyone shows him great affection. The hugs and cuddles he received just then were unbelievable. When she finally broke off, his new American pal summoned her friends across for photographs.

I offered to take their pictures and then we chatted amiably about what a wonderful time they were having on their tour. For all my misgivings, because frankly, it seemed quite mad to travel halfway across the world to meet a dog, she and her companions were brilliant and I felt privileged to have spent time in their company. On the way home, with Max and Paddy riding alongside me, I realised just what a powerful effect our canine friends can have. Our connection with dogs is quite remarkable. Whatever it is we seek from them, whether it's comfort, companionship or fun, they are always there for us, no matter how far we come to find it.

With people flocking from far and wide to meet Max and Paddy, and the numbers steadily building, I realised I had to do something to make it manageable. I didn't want to turn anyone down, or claim I was too busy, but the fact remained I had a mobile locksmith business to run. As Angela and I continued to have lunch at the same cafe every day, and enjoyed our time there together, I decided on a simple solution: if anyone wanted to drop in and say hi to the dogs on the one-lunchtime-per-week, we would be happy to see them.

We met a lot of nice people this way and even made some good friends. It was a lovely way to spend an hour. They came for all sorts of reasons. Some were simply fans of Springer Spaniels and often brought their dogs with them. They'd be absolutely besotted with their dogs, as I am with mine, and it was lovely to bond over this shared experience. Others just found a spark of joy in seeing pictures of Max and Paddy romping around the Lake District and often they would share their stories with us. We heard tales of mental and physical health issues, loneliness and anxiety. Often our visitors would say that reading about my own experience had given them the courage to admit they weren't coping, and that moved me very deeply. If Max and Paddy were the key to unlocking lives in this way, it gave me renewed purpose in celebrating their lives and adventures online.

It's here that I have to mention one very special lady called Diane. Her daughter wrote to me with a story about how her mother sought comfort in keeping up with my dogs' escapades while living with terminal cancer. It moved me very deeply. She explained that even with limited time available, her mum, Diane, did not believe in grand bucket lists. Instead, she considered life to be the most precious gift of all, and something to celebrate from start to finish. With this in mind, her daughter asked if I would be willing to create a simple memory for her mum, and together we put a plan into place.

One Sunday morning, on a trip to the Lake District, her husband took her on a mystery visit to the beautiful, dramatic stone circles at Castlerigg, with views across to Helvellyn Mountain and High Seat. There, unbeknownst to Diane, I was waiting with two boys who meant so much to her. Afterwards, shortly before she passed away, Diane wrote to me about the experience. Not only did I come to treasure that note, it led to me to reconsider how much time I spent on the road as a locksmith. I loved my new career, but life was just so precious. We crossed the road and ventured the short distance to the stone circle. Diane said on describing the moments after she had been introduced to Max and Paddy: 'How magical it was … the serenity of the hills, the light of the sun streaming through the fragments of clouds and the calming of the Stones. I'd never felt so happy and contented as of that moment in time. Everything else happening in my life just left me, as if I'd stepped through a parallel portal to another world. Never having owned dogs in my life, it felt that these two were mine.'

On many occasions, people would also ask if they could join us on a dog walk. I would be happy to agree when I could, but frankly, the increasing number of requests led many to be disappointed. This really weighed heavily on my shoulders. At the same time, our weekly meet and greets would often see five, 10 or 15 people turn up at the table.

'We need to do something,' I said to Angela on the way home one afternoon, after Max and Paddy had been so mobbed by affection that we didn't even have a chance to eat. 'Meeting the dogs makes people happy, but the cafe will kick us out if this carries on.'

'So, why don't you make it the start of something bigger?' she suggested.

I glanced across at her – Paddy was getting quite large to be sitting on her lap now.

'Like what?'

Paddy peered over his shoulder at her. Angela smiled and patted his flank.

'An event,' she said simply. 'For charity.'

* * *

We arrived back at the house with the spark of an idea. It was one I could not stop thinking about over the days and weeks that followed. Over long lunchtime chats, Angela and I devised a way for as many people as possible to meet Max and Paddy, and at the same time make a contribution to a cause close to our hearts. I had never organised anything on this scale before, and so my first task was to find a suitable place for everyone to gather. I settled on a cafe with a walled kitchen garden in the grounds of the Lingholm Estate. It's such a serene, warm and friendly location overlooking Derwentwater, and I was so grateful to the folks there for their blessing and support.

With the venue sorted, I posted an invitation on Max and Paddy's Facebook page. It was really quite vague as I wasn't sure what the response would be like. I just asked if anyone would be interested in joining a dog walk to raise funds for a local rescue centre, with a view to starting at the cafe.

By the end of the day, just before Facebook temporarily froze the page as it looked like it was being spammed, I had received over 800 replies.

The response was overwhelming. It took me completely by surprise. Aware that even my chosen cafe couldn't cope with that sort of number, I limited the event to 75 places. It still seemed like a lot, but I worried about it all going wrong. My plan was to walk from the cafe gardens to the lake shore. It was a route I had done many times before, taking us through a bluebell wood and across two fields to a bridge. Along with Max and Paddy, and with one eye on my surroundings to basically make sure it would be safe and accessible for everyone, it took me an hour to make it there and back. I decided that 90 minutes should be plenty of time for a small crowd of dog lovers to enjoy the experience and sent out a message to everyone attending to start gathering at the cafe a good hour beforehand. With plenty of parking available, and a chance to enjoy a delicious lunch beforehand, Angela and I hoped it would be a nice afternoon for all involved and a chance to give something back to our local community.

Then the big day arrived, bright and bathed in sunshine, and my confidence wobbled.

'What if nobody shows up?' I whispered to Angela. We were at our table at the cafe, with Max and Paddy sitting dutifully at our feet. It's a popular venue and always busy. Looking around, inside and out on the terrace, customers were enjoying their lunch as ever. Some had dogs with them as well, but that wasn't unusual. I leaned across the table so I couldn't be overheard.

'Maybe I made a mistake with the dates on the invite?'

'Kerry,' said Angela, finishing her salad, 'we still have 10 minutes to go. Just enjoy your lunch for now.'

But I couldn't finish my meal, I was too nervous. Instead, I sipped at my glass of water with one eye on the clock. All I could think was that if we had made a massive mistake here, we could just leave and nobody would notice.

'Are you ready?' I said when the time came.

'Are *you*?' asked Angela.

I glanced under the table. Whatever happened, Max and Paddy were peering up at me, ready for their walk.

'I'm in good company,' I said and rose from the table. 'Come on, then.'

As we stood up, just for a moment, a hush fell over the cafe. Then, before I could register what was going on, people began to rise from their tables. Dogs stood up and began to wag their tails excitedly while their owners clambered into their coats. It was the same out on the terrace, where several dogs started barking with excitement.

I looked at Angela, barely able to believe what was going on here.

'Congratulations,' she said. 'Now, let Max and Paddy take everyone on a walk they won't forget.'

People had come from near and far. As we set off, I met visitors who came from Devon in the south and all the way from the north of Scotland. It was incredible and proved to me that social media really can be a force for good. I had banked on 80 people attending, but hadn't considered that many would bring family and friends. So, what was a simple walk had become an event for over 120 and one that raised funds for a shelter that provided a valuable service in caring for dogs in need of a home. Max and Paddy were stars from start to finish. They led the way and with such gusto that all their new four-legged friends followed suit. All the dogs were a credit to their owners as well, which just made the whole event so memorable and pleasurable.

Our first charity walk went with just one hitch, and that was my timing. I had vastly underestimated how long it would take to shepherd a group intent on making the most of this lovely neck of the woods to the bridge and back.

Throw a whole bunch of fun-loving dogs into the mix, many of whom followed Max and Paddy into the water down by the shoreline, and it was no surprise that my 90-minute ramble lasted for much of the afternoon. It was without doubt a very late finish, and could not have been more of a success.

25

Star Springers

LIFE WAS GOOD. I loved my second career as a mobile locksmith and relished time with Angela. Max and Paddy had become the best of friends, and although different in their personalities, they fitted together like two jigsaw pieces. Their Facebook page continued to grow, while our charity walks from the Lingholm became a regular feature on the canine calendar.

It was a challenge to manage numbers, of course. I wanted each event to be pleasurable for everyone. That meant working closely with the cafe and also caring for the environment. When more than 100 people and their dogs were rambling across the countryside it was vital to me that everyone did so respectfully and came back feeling enriched by the experience.

Our walks continued to raise money for local causes, with people coming from far and wide to take part. Local hotels and guest houses were happy about that, as was the local tourism association. They even branded Max and Paddy official canine ambassadors to Keswick, which was a step up for my head of security and his restless apprentice.

Sure enough, this attracted the attention of the local press, which included a short piece for regional television news. It was all good fun and I was so proud of my boys. They really were making a difference through their simple joy for life. Naturally, the camera focused on them and I was quite happy with that while I talked to the reporter about their walks for good causes. Then came the question I had answered once before but which I still found hard to handle.

'Tell me about the accident. I read an article in which you revealed it led to a period of depression.'

Talking about mental-health issues can feel deeply exposing. You feel vulnerable and open to judgement, yet the more I opened up about it, the easier it became. Nobody judged me. In fact, I received nothing but support from well-wishers via Max and Paddy's Facebook page, along with a steady stream of messages from people who felt empowered by my experience and ready to face up to their own personal challenges.

We all love dogs for different reasons. I have always just liked to have them by my side, but without a doubt meeting Max was a form of therapy that saved me. I had been hesitant in putting this into words when the journalist from the local magazine first asked me about it. After that was published, when people approached me about it on charity walks and Facebook, I found myself making more sense of it as I retold my story. This time, despite suddenly feeling very self-conscious in front of a television camera, I tried to be as open as I could about just what I had been through over those dark and crushing years. It was tough, but I felt like I had done the right thing. I knew that if I could open up, as an ordinary man who had found salvation through his dogs, then perhaps that would speak to other people. I just wanted to show that there is always hope, no matter how bleak things can be, and sometimes that comes in the shape of animals that look to us with nothing but loyalty and love.

Sure enough, when the news item went out, the Facebook feed kicked into overdrive. Yet more people recognised me by my dogs, stopped me in the street or out on walks, and asked to shake my hand. Some revealed they were suffering from personal issues themselves, or just recognised that it took guts for me to talk about what I'd been through. Whatever the case, everyone loved to meet Max and Paddy. They became easier to recognise as a duo and not a walk went by without someone making a beeline towards me because my dogs looked familiar.

As star Springers, which is how Angela and I often joked about them, Paddy's big break came when he was seven months old. ITV called me because they were making a programme called *Britain's Favourite Walks: Top 100*. The researcher had seen the news piece and explored the Facebook page, and wondered if I would be interested in nominating a walk of note that my dogs and I particularly enjoyed. Of all the routes I considered, I knew it had to be Catbells. It just meant so much to me and I will never forget that moment on the churchyard bench when I dreamed that one day I would take Max to the viewing point overlooking the lake.

A week before filming, it rained incessantly. I pictured Paddy, Max and I slopping through the mud on the steep rise up from the stream and doubted it would make attractive television. Then, on the morning the crew travelled to meet us, the rain stopped and the sun broke through. It shaped up to be a beautiful day, with cotton wool clouds floating over the hilltops. I arranged to meet the producer down by the lakeshore. He arrived by minibus along with the film crew and didn't look very happy when he climbed out.

'I bloody hate walking!' he announced, only half-joking as he shook my hand. 'And I also can't stand dogs!'

'Oh,' I said, as Max and Paddy sploshed around behind me. 'Let's see if we can change your mind about that.'

In total, for what would be a fairly short segment in the show, we filmed for about seven hours. Max and Paddy were brilliant. They frolicked on cue, or walked obediently to heel, and generally entertained the crew. It was really tiring, with lots of retakes as I talked about what the walk meant to me and how inspirational I found it. When we finally wrapped, I accompanied the producer back to his waiting taxi.

'Do you know what?' he said to me. 'This has been one of the best days of my career. The weather has been stunning and your dogs are amazing.'

'All dogs are amazing,' I said. 'They can do you the power of good.'

The producer chuckled as he climbed into the passenger seat.

'Normally, I'm filming neighbours from hell,' he said. 'Give me your Spaniels any day of the week. They look at you as if you're a god.'

'Maybe I am,' I said cheekily, though when I came to share this with Angela she didn't quite see it that way.

Like everyone involved in the show, I had no idea where our walk would rank in the Top 100. I sat down to watch and held my breath with every stop-off on the countdown. I'd assumed we'd be somewhere near the bottom. With no mention of us on reaching number 75, I told Max and Paddy that anywhere from here would be a triumph. Then the show reached the halfway mark and I began to wonder whether we had even made the cut.

'Never mind,' said Angela. 'At least you had a nice day.'

'We had a lovely time,' I agreed and silently began to question whether I should have kept quiet about our contribution on the Facebook feed.

When the Top 20 arrived, I felt certain we had been edited out of the show completely. As the Top 10 got underway, I was ready to switch it off and head for bed.

'Just wait,' said Angela. 'Never give up hope. Isn't that right?'

As we watched the fifth most popular walk, I was all ready to tell her that I could make an exception here and with no desire to be famous, that was fine by me.

Then came number four. I saw myself on the screen, along with Max and Paddy as we hiked the trail, and simply stared at the screen in shock.

I still couldn't believe it the next morning when I sat down in front of the Facebook page and saw just how many people had seen us. All through the week, it seemed as if everyone I knew had watched the show, and that's when things went crazy.

When I first moved to Keswick, joining Angela in the town that has been our home for decades, I never dreamed that one year I would be asked to switch on the Christmas lights. Strictly speaking, it wasn't me who carried out the honour, but I was present on stage.

When the invitation arrived, inviting Max and Paddy to be the star turn, I assumed it would be a small ceremonial event with a photographer from the local paper and my wife out of shot, keeping me grounded. Shortly after I accepted on behalf of the dogs, I realised I had underestimated the scale of the occasion.

'This is the third time the press have called me for an interview,' I said to Angela in the days leading up to the event. 'People on Facebook are even talking about travelling across the country for it.'

'I was in town this morning,' she said. 'Have you seen the stage they're building on the square?'

I felt a little bit sick when she told me this. Fortunately, whenever I faced a daunting task in the spotlight, I knew that Max and Paddy would always draw attention away from me.

'Don't let me down, boys,' I said. 'All you have to do is flick a switch.'

Fortunately, one of the technical guys with more brains than me realised that dogs aren't that dexterous. So, rather than present Max and Paddy with a lever, the organisers asked me to bring them to a rehearsal room in Cockermouth so they could try out the proposed solution.

'It's a box,' I said, as they unveiled the dog-friendly device.

'Not just any box.' The technician in charge invited Max to jump on top. Max looked at me. I gave him the nod and he duly obliged. At once, thanks to the lights rigged up inside, the box turned red. 'See!' he said proudly. 'It's pressure sensitive.'

'Amazing,' I said, as Max jumped off and Paddy had a go. 'And that will turn on the Christmas lights?'

'No, I'll do that from a switch,' he said, which was rather deflating but I could appreciate the magic would be there for the good people of Keswick. 'It's going to be great!'

On the day of the event, I felt increasingly twitchy. I didn't dare pop down to the square to see preparations. With so many people saying they were coming, from friends and neighbours to fans of the Facebook page, I pretty much pretended it wasn't happening. Eventually, as the sun began to set, I couldn't avoid it any longer. I gave Max and Paddy a good brush and reminded them both of their duties.

'One of you just has to jump on the box, that's it. It doesn't matter who does it, but Christmas in Keswick is depending on this.'

Ever since Paddy joined Max, people sometimes assume I named them both after the central characters from a popular Channel 4 sitcom *Max and Paddy's Road to Nowhere* by the comedian Peter Kay. It's just a coincidence, but on this occasion, I learned from the Facebook page that some lads from Newcastle had misunderstood who would be switching on the lights and hired a van to be here. As a result, with little time to go before my dogs walked on stage, they were now in town in the hope of seeing their comedy idol and his ensemble.

I felt awful for them and it did little for my confidence. Checking my appearance in the mirror before I left the house, I was so pale it looked like I was coming down with the flu.

'It's just nerves,' Angela assured me as she climbed into her coat. 'Everything will be fine when you get down there.'

Along the way, with Max and Paddy on leads, we bumped into a woman from our street. She was walking up from the direction of the town square. I stopped to ask how things were shaping up.

'There are a few people down there,' she told me.

I turned to Angela.

'That doesn't sound good. Shall we just turn around and pretend this never happened?'

My wife linked her arm through mine.

'Come on,' she said, 'we can't be late.'

The route down to the square winds along several different roads. With every turn, it seemed like more and more people were heading in the same direction. Either our neighbour had underestimated the numbers, I thought to myself, or another event was going on in Keswick that evening. Judging by the rate at which their tails switched back and forth, Max and Paddy seemed aware that something exciting was happening. It was only as we turned the corner into the square, however, and came to a halt because of the sheer size of the crowd in front of the stage, that I was forced to face the facts.

Max and Paddy were set to switch on the Christmas lights, and people had flocked here to celebrate the occasion with them. With stalls for the winter market laden with goods, and a big tree resplendent at the heart of it all, the atmosphere seemed both magical and terrifying.

It took a while to squeeze our way around the edge of the throng to reach the guest area. There, we were greeted by our friendly technician, along with the host for the event.

'Which one is going to jump on the box?' asked the host before we climbed the steps to the stage. He turned to look down at Max and Paddy, who peered up as if perhaps he might have a treat for them.

'Let's make it a surprise,' I said, because frankly I had no idea.

We walked out to a big cheer. My knees felt like they had turned to curls of butter. With the boys showing no sign of stage fright, I struggled through a quick interview. Then, as the spotlight fell on Max and Paddy, I took a step back and joined in with the countdown from 10. It was Paddy who had my eye throughout. I clicked my fingers at the right time and gestured towards the box. With a roar from the audience, he jumped straight on. The technical guy then took his cue and within a blink, the town square was ablaze in twinkling Christmas lights.

It was awesome.

When Paddy jumped down, I hugged him tight and drew Max in for a cuddle. They had done so well and now they had the community behind them. Our host announced that if anyone wanted to meet the dogs in person then they could do so in a courtyard on the opposite side of the square. As we prepared to climb offstage and make our way there, I noticed a little girl holding two stuffed toy dogs. I smiled and waved before following a security guy who led us safely through to the courtyard.

We had a fabulous time meeting so many people. Even the lads from Newcastle showed up to say hello. Having discovered that Max and Paddy weren't Peter Kay characters but Springer Spaniels, they had piled into the nearest pub in high spirits and – bar the driver – proceeded to get blotto. They were good fun and it was a pleasure to meet them, along with everyone who queued to meet the boys. Even the little girl with the two toy dogs showed up with her mother. She sat with Max and stroked his ear for about 15 minutes. I was mindful that others were waiting to meet them, but she seemed entranced.

'She takes those toy dogs everywhere,' said her mum, when she finally coaxed her away. 'They're called Max and Paddy.'

Early the next morning, via Facebook, I received a message that moved me deeply. It was from the mother of the little girl, thanking me for giving her so much time in Max's company. I replied to say it had been a great pleasure and sent her a calendar of the dogs that I had made that year.

A few days later, her mother sent me a short clip of her daughter looking through the photographs for every month of the year with wide-eyed wonder. It was lovely, and in the correspondence that followed, I learned that this little girl had been falling behind at school. She was dyslexic, and her struggle with reading and writing had led to her being picked on. It had rocked her confidence, causing her eczema to flare, but she'd found comfort in these two stuffed toy dogs that she'd named as a fan of the Facebook page. A week later, her mother wrote to me again to say that her daughter had written a poem about meeting Max. Not only that, it had won a prize in a local competition, which was such a thrill to me. By her mum's account, it was one more stepping stone in her daughter's road to becoming her old self again and she credited my dogs for helping her. Together with her younger brother, this sweet little girl and their mother joined me on a walk one day. She even showed up with her two toys peeping out of her rucksack. It was lovely and such a joy to see her come alive with Max and Paddy.

Sometime later, her mother told me that they'd taken on a Springer Spaniel puppy. It had been the making of her daughter, she said, and within days, her eczema had vanished.

How nice is that?

26

The Notorious
Brown Leg Gang

IN THE SUMMER OF 2018, with a string of charity walks under their collars, Max and Paddy were nominated for an award that moved me to tears. It came from the People's Dispensary for Sick Animals, or PDSA for short, which is a veterinary charity that provides care for sick or injured animals belonging to owners experiencing financial hardship. The nomination for the PDSA's Commendation Award came in the form of a letter. It recognised Max and Paddy for human devotion and enriching the lives of others. Not only had Max helped me back from the brink, so it said, the charity wanted to celebrate their work as 'virtual therapy dogs' in terms of the joy and comfort they brought so many people via their Facebook page.

The ceremony was held in a hotel in Penrith, with more than 70 guests. Many of them were fans of Max and Paddy, who had stories of their own to tell. One woman had lost her son and found solace in a dog, which was in attendance with her, while my little friend with the two toy pups was there with her mum. My dogs might have been commended on that day, but really it is an award that celebrates the connection with all our canine friends.

By now, I had told my story enough times to feel more comfortable about being so open. No longer a closed-off individual, with his feelings under lock and key, I wore my emotions close to the surface. In fact, I could become a mess without hesitation. I was also quite happy to be like this. It felt freeing, and I credited Max and Paddy for helping me to make that transformation. I had also seen the impact this had on people experiencing their own personal difficulties. If an ordinary bloke like me could own his depression and the dogs that helped him overcome it then anyone could tell their story. Dogs are also great icebreakers, I find. After the ceremony, people came up to talk to me but the focus was on Max and Paddy. For some that made it easier for them to address sensitive or personal issues. I often found people playing with the dogs while sharing the most heartbreaking stories and then finishing with a smile. Their problems weren't solved, of course, but this first step towards addressing things, with the help of two soppy Spaniels, gave them hope.

At the same time, Max and Paddy's Facebook page had taken on a life of its own. With so many people contributing, it had become a thriving community. Not only that, it revolved around positive values. Everyone came to the page to see two dogs loving life in a beautiful part of the country and that provided them with a little boost. While I understood the power of the page, I didn't pretend to be some kind of miracle worker. My role was to keep on posting nice photographs and videos, and sharing the love I felt for my dear Springers. I didn't make a big deal about the breed, any dog with a kind heart can form a bond with someone in a time of need. So, when I was approached by ITV once more, about a programme called *Britain's Top 100 Dogs*, I was happy for them to feature Max and Paddy purely to help spread the word about canine therapy.

Once again, a film crew travelled up to the Lakes and my dogs proved themselves to be small-screen stars by jetty jumping for the camera and then frolicking over the hillsides with a drone filming them from overhead. It was another good day, and a great experience, but I came home with no expectation that we would match the success of *Britain's Favourite Walks: Top 100*.

Springer Spaniels have been a part of my life since I was a young man. It's a breed that I have come to love for their sense of sheer joy, constant companionship and the intense bond they can build. What I hadn't considered was the fact that the general population of dog lovers would also recognise and appreciate these qualities.

On the night the show went out live, I experienced that weird out-of-body experience on seeing myself on the television with Max and Paddy. It took a while for me to register that the Springer Spaniel came in as the nation's fourth favourite breed of dog. Once we were into the Top 10, I'd considered any placing to be a great result, and frankly, when the countdown began for the last five, I found the stress too much to bear. I couldn't believe it, but in a sense it proved to me that I wasn't alone: the whole country, it seemed, saw something magical and restorative in a breed devoted to living life to the full. In the days after the show went out, as well as being stopped in the street by complete strangers who wanted to shake my hand for speaking up about depression, I received over 10,000 messages via the Facebook page from people who recognised that dogs really can save lives.

I felt so blessed to have Max and Paddy. They defined my days and kept me company wherever I went. I couldn't have wished for any more from my dogs, which is why I knew that Angela would be aghast when I decided that what I needed was one more.

'I can't explain it,' I reasoned. 'It just feels like three would make the most brilliant gang.'

Even as I addressed it with my wife, having plucked up the courage this time, I could see her mentally writing off the chance of a clean kitchen floor for some months. We were just doing up the house as well. My timing could not have been worse.

'Kerry, I just don't know.'

I had expected Angela to rule out another dog without question. Instead, she reacted with bafflement and also hesitation. It was a chink of light, rather than a closed door. I was determined to bring her round.

'I nearly forgot,' I said, and produced a gift-wrapped package for her. 'Max and Paddy have got you a present.'

Angela knew full well where this was going. I knew I couldn't buy her approval, I just wanted to show that I appreciated the fact that she tolerated my crazy devotion to these dogs.

'Is this a bribe?' she asked, unwrapping the box. 'I can't be bribed … oh, a new iPhone!'

It was word from the breeder responsible for Paddy that had persuaded me to give it a shot. She told me that she planned to produce one more litter from his mother, Molly. That was enough for me to put my name down for a pup. It would be a little brother for Paddy, and one more protégé for Max to bring up to speed.

Within minutes of firing up her new phone, Angela was googling names for the new arrival. I knew I wanted another boy, it just seemed to fit. Once the litter arrived, all we needed to do was pick the pup. When the breeder called me to arrange a time, she said jokingly that she already knew which one I'd choose.

'I'm going to leave that to Angela,' I told her, because this time I wanted her to be involved.

Over time, my wife had come round to life with Springer Spaniels. Yes, it could be hectic and high energy, but in amongst the madness was love and devotion, and that wasn't lost on her.

'How about this chap?' said Angela, cradling a pup in her arms. We had arrived just as some of these little scraps opened their eyes for the very first time. 'He has a brown leg, just like Paddy.'

I glanced at the breeder, who smiled as if to say this was precisely the reason she felt he was destined to join us.

Angela handed me the little one. At my feet, a whole bunch of puppies were clamouring for attention. I cuddled him close to my chest. Like my wife, I couldn't ignore the fact that he did indeed share the same striking mark as his older brother.

'Do we pick you?' I asked, levelling with his face.

The pup licked my nose, and that was that.

Both Max and Paddy have always struck me as solid, handsome names. I didn't want to call the new dog something random like Spud or Dave; I also knew that if he was anything like the other two, then he had a big responsibility on his shoulders. In the weeks before he joined us, Angela and I chewed over what we should call him. It's a big thing, I think. Do you choose a name that suits a puppy, one he'll grow into, or something that matches his character, perhaps? Eventually, on the day we visited him, we came up with a name we both agreed would be fitting. With people on Facebook messaging me constantly to find out, I posted a picture of our sweet new arrival with some thoughts about his future.

Max has been my king of the Lakes, my saviour and the light in many people's lives. Paddy Padawan joined us as his apprentice and has taken to his role faster than he can destroy a charity shop toy. We are immensely proud of them both, what they have become and what they do.

Our new puppy opened his eyes on his naming day. Hopefully, he will see so much in his life. He may be small but has all the world to grow into.

We've given him a name of a prince who has inspired many thousands of people across the globe, both young and old. This is a man who has spoken openly about his depression and mental health issues. He's someone who has helped and inspired thousands of wounded servicemen and women suffering from PTSD, that they should be given the respect they deserve, and enabled to lead fulfilling lives.

Our pup will be named after Prince Harry. Could our little man inspire just one person to talk openly about depression, or make a lonely soul smile and feel wanted? Or what if he inspires one child to put down their phone and get outdoors to create a real life-changing adventure?

Our new puppy joined Max and Paddy just after Christmas that year. Harry had his own bed alongside the others, but within no time they were mixing and matching. Sometimes I would find Harry snoring on his back with his paws in the air in Max's bed, while Max and Paddy had curled up together. On other occasions, especially after a long walk across the fells, I would find them all in a heap in the same bed. This trio of crazy Springers formed a tight bond and I felt so privileged to be at the heart of it.

Harry didn't stay little for long. Even as a puppy, he put on the pounds at an impressive rate to become a strong, lively, curious and noble young dog. He's a sweet-natured soul with a big heart and paws who has already become an ambassador for the PDSA. The boys are often invited to visit schools and there my Harry comes into his own. He's so gentle with children, especially those unfamiliar with dogs, and allows them to gain their confidence simply by sitting quietly as they stroke him and then chat as if they've just made a friend for life.

Harry has learned everything from Max and Paddy, of course, from the skills he needs to be a therapy dog to the fine art of jetty jumping. At first, he was reluctant to get in the water. He hovered around the edge, watching with interest as his partners in crime paddled around in big circles. Finally, one day, he summoned the courage to follow them in. Now, he adores it so much, he's often the first to take the plunge.

When it comes to having his photograph taken, Harry is a natural. He'll always find his place with the other two, from sitting on a bench to standing proud on a hillside, and it's been lovely to watch him grow from a little scrap to the largest of the three. As a trio, they just seem to fit. On walks, once they've piled out of the van, all three set off ahead but constantly shuttle back to check on me. They're just so full of life and alert to their surroundings. I might not be able to bound after them at their pace, but it's always a joyful experience.

I aim to photograph them on every walk. Whenever I produce my smartphone to line up a picture they swing together like a slightly uncoordinated but hyperactive acrobatic troupe, and I continue to be amazed at the public response to the shots I take. I can post a picture on their Facebook page and thousands of people will respond by pressing 'like'. Whether they've been briefly amused by Max's tenacity at hauling a wide stick through a narrow space, or sought a moment of escape, I know from personal experience that dogs can make a difference. It's still very raw for me, in fact. I feel sad when I think about how my life might have ended if I hadn't met Max. I'm a completely different person than I was before the accident. The salesman driven to achieving targets has gone. I'm happier now and at peace with my childhood. People sometimes say that

I showed Max how to shine in life, but the fact is he did that for me.

In a world that can sometimes seem like a dark place, our canine companions offer nothing but love, devotion, joy and hope. For me, Max, Paddy and Harry bring light into my life and I hope that light continues to keep shining for others. Whether it's this trio of four-legged fell runners or any dog, from the finest pedigree to the wandering street mutt, there's a connection waiting to happen and that can last a lifetime – it's just a question of reaching out.

27

From the Yard to the Palace

PADDY AND HARRY HAVE HELPED MAX to take our charity walks from strength to strength. We've organised a whole host of different outings, all raising money for good causes, and they continue to grow in popularity. I love seeing so many people and their dogs come together. In general, it's a Springer Spaniel thing, but every breed is welcome. Even Pugs!

Incredibly, over the years the boys have raised over £90,000 for charity. I always get choked up when I think about what a force for good they have become, and their achievements have not gone unrecognised.

'Ange,' I called up to my wife one morning, having just picked up the post. I held a letter in my hand with an impressive coat of arms and an invitation that left me stunned, 'we've been invited to Buckingham Palace!'

'What?' That was enough to coax her away from her work. 'You're joking!'

I showed her the letter from the Office of the Lord Lieutenant, summoning Angela and me to the Royal Garden Party in recognition of our fundraising efforts.

'I'm thrilled,' I said as she read it for herself. 'But there's no mention that the dogs are invited.'

'It's not Crufts, Kerry.'

Already, I could feel myself getting separation anxiety. Max had been with me every day since I had officially become his owner, while Paddy and Harry had never known life without me. We had even been to Crufts, and did so as a team.

'I'm not sure I want to go,' I confessed. 'Not without Max. If it wasn't for him, we'd never have raised a penny.'

Angela studied the invite.

'Well, it doesn't say he can't come with us,' she said.

I decided to call the office that had sent out the invitation. Over the phone, I spoke to a very nice lady with a cut-glass accent who listened politely when I asked if I could bring my dog.

'Is he a working dog?' she asked. 'With a uniform?'

I told her Max was a qualified therapy dog and did indeed own a smart red jacket for the role.

'Does that count?' I asked hopefully and was delighted when she confirmed that it did. After making some enquiries, she called me back and all of a sudden, our invitation effectively had a plus one.

It was a shame that I couldn't bring Paddy and Harry too, but I understood. They're both still young and I have no doubt one day their moment will come, but this was all about Max. I felt a lot better about leaving them behind once I had arranged for them to stay with their mum, Moll. I'd stayed in touch with the breeder and we'd ended up becoming good friends. When the big day dawned, we set off early to drop them off and settle them in. I knew they would be in good hands. In fact, I figured they'd have the time of their lives.

That left me, Angela and Max to drive to Penrith and catch a train down to London. I had it all planned out, with plenty of time built into the schedule so we didn't have to stress.

'There are no spaces,' I said to Angela as we cruised around the long-stay car park by the railway station. My knuckles had turned white where I gripped the steering wheel, having spent the best part of an hour longer than anticipated in traffic. 'What are we going to do?'

'Stay calm,' she said. 'We can easily park across town and then get a taxi.'

Half an hour later, as we sat in the back of a stationary cab while the driver tried in vain to release a malfunctioning automatic handbrake, I had all but given up hope. As Angela dialled for another taxi, I looked at Max. He was sitting patiently beside me, showing no sign that he shared our stress. Yet again, his calming presence helped me to stay grounded. If we failed to make it, I thought to myself, we could have a nice long walk instead. As Angela had packed her finest outfit, however, I knew that giving up was not an option.

We caught the train with minutes to spare. I'd booked us tickets in advance and chosen a table seat so that we could all enjoy the view together. Max was in his element. It was a step up from the van, with the added bonus that people on their way to the buffet car would stop to make a fuss of him. There's nothing like a dog to break the ice on a journey and Max loved every minute.

On the journey down, I read out messages of support on the Facebook page. Having shared the news we were off to the Palace, the responses went off the scale. There was just so much love for my little dog, and also interest from the press. In fact, once we'd arrived at the station and checked into the dog-friendly hotel where we'd be staying overnight, we were met by a reporter for a national newspaper. They had asked to cover the story of Max's trip. I saw it as a chance to increase awareness of Max's good work, which could only help in boosting future fundraising.

By now, Angela and I were both beginning to feel quite nervous. We had dressed up in our room and Max was sporting his bright red jacket. It had been a long time since I wore a tie. I didn't feel comfortable at all and wished I could carry myself as elegantly as Angela. She looked lovely in her polka-dot dress. The reporter travelled with us by black cab to the Palace. On the way, she told me the best place to stand in the garden for a view of the Royal Family members when they appeared for the meet and greet. It felt like insider information we could put to good use.

When the Palace swung into view, and we climbed out at the gate for garden party visitors, I hadn't realised we would be in such illustrious company. There were thousands of people, all in their finery, each invited for their contribution to society. It was humbling to be amongst them, but once again, Max proved to be the presence that sparked chatter and conversation. We met lots of people, some of whom were familiar with the Facebook page, and that included the Mounted Police. Max had his photo taken beside some handsome-looking horses and their riders. We were also met by a photographer from the paper. He asked me to kneel beside Max, with the Palace gates behind us. It was such a proud moment, but one cut short when I felt something give in the sole of my foot.

'What's wrong?' asked Angela as I muttered to myself and made a meal of standing up again.

'It's my shoe,' I whispered, and then turned away from the photographer as he examined his shots to show her the problem I had.

I'm used to wearing sturdy walking boots, not dress shoes. I'd kept an old pair from my sales conference days, but can only think they had deteriorated over time. I wiggled my foot for Angela once again. The sole of the shoe had come away at the toes, and now yawned and flapped like a loose jaw.

'Can you tape it?' she asked.

'With what?' I spread my hands, only to break into an obliging smile as the photographer asked for one more shot.

Shortly afterwards, we began to file in through the security checks. I did so with a pained-looking shuffle. All of a sudden, with a support dog at my side, it looked like Max was here for an entirely different reason. Resigned to the fact that I had acquired a limp for the day, with Angela smirking beside me, I had seen the funny side by the time we stepped out into the sunshine again.

The Royal Garden was magnificent. I felt like I had walked into an oasis in the heart of the city and took a moment just looking around at the exquisite landscaping and the sprawling lake, where swans sailed serenely.

'Can you believe this?' I said to Angela as we mingled beneath a beating sun. 'I feel like we're trespassing.'

My wife reached down and patted Max on his flank. He looked so handsome in his jacket and a far cry from the lonely yard dog I had chanced upon so long ago.

'He deserves to be here,' she said. 'You both do.'

We decide to follow the advice of our correspondent friend and make our way to the spot that would give us the best view when the Royal Family members joined the Garden Party. Hobbling along, trying hard not to let my shoe sole flap, I caught the eye of a Chelsea Pensioner.

'Make way,' he said, stepping out into the crowd to help me. 'Can we create some space for this gentleman and his dog.'

I didn't like to say why I was walking in such an arduous fashion. I just accepted his help with thanks, grasped Max's leash tightly and avoided Angela's eye in case either of us got the giggles.

The reporter was right about the spot she recommended: it gave us a clear view. With just minutes to go before the Royals were due to emerge, a lady with a clipboard approached Angela and me. I assumed she was going to request that we move. Instead, she registered Max with a glance and then ticked something off a list.

'You're to be presented,' she told me. 'Follow me.'

Lost for words, but aware that we were the only people there with a dog and so there could have been no mistake, Angela and I did as we were told.

It was then, standing apart from the rest of the invited guests, alongside just a handful selected to meet our Royal hosts, that I began to feel panicky. I was so used to being in my own little world up in the Lakes, and now here I was set to meet royalty. I was clasping Max's lead so tightly, and just then it felt like I couldn't function without him. The fact that he had settled at my feet, hiding my shoe malfunction, and appeared to have nodded off made no difference to me. He was still here as a source of strength. I glanced at Angela – she looked just as out of her depth. Then all eyes turned to a small party that emerged from the Palace just then. At the centre were two figures in their finery and Angela's face lit up.

'It's Prince William and Catherine,' I told Max under my breath, as if that might bring him to his feet. 'Moo, wake up!'

When Max had first poked his nose through the yard railings to get my attention, I'd had no idea that we were about to embark on a journey that would take us here. Had I known, I would've been as shell-shocked as I felt after the Duke and Duchess of Cambridge moved on from us. The lady with the clipboard had told me we could expect to be in conversation for no more than a minute. I'm told our chat lasted four times that length. In that time, to great interest and compassion from the Royal couple, I explained how Max had effectively saved me from the grip of depression and had gone on to help others with mental-health issues. The fact that he remained conked out in the sun as we talked was quite fitting, I thought. Even Prince William observed that he was the most laid-back Spaniel he had ever met.

The exchange was wonderful. It also left me feeling emotionally wrung out. In fact, moments after the Royal couple moved on, I burst into tears. All of a sudden I found myself surrounded by concerned guests, from military personnel to charity workers, who had no clue that I could cry at a change in the weather. Later, as we left along with everyone else, still scraping one foot along the ground as I went, the journalist from the newspaper met us outside.

'How did it go?' she asked, ready to capture our story.

I drew breath to begin and then, overwhelmed by where my adventure with Max had just taken me, promptly dissolved into tears once again.

The next morning, after a long sleep at the hotel to recover from the emotion of the day, Angela, Max and I climbed into a black cab for the station. The cab driver didn't seem thrilled to have a dog on board, and asked me to make sure he stayed on the floor in front of the seat. It wasn't a long journey, but the traffic was bad and before too long we started talking. The driver had a few things to say about a news item on the radio, and then mentioned that he'd read a story in the paper that morning about a dog attending a garden party at Buckingham Palace.

'It was a Springer, I think,' he chuckled. 'Like yours.'

'This is the dog.' I exchanged a glance with Angela. 'Say hello to Max.'

The driver caught my eye in the rear-view mirror, took a moment to process things and then beamed at me.

'Well, it's an honour,' he said. 'Max can sit on the seat if he wants.'

I assured him that Max was fine at my feet, where he had somehow settled in for a snooze.

'He had a busy day yesterday,' I explained. 'As I'm sure you can imagine.'

'He deserves to rest,' said the driver, 'and all credit to you for having the guts to speak up about what you went through. Most blokes I know just stick their heads in the sand.'

I thanked him for his kind words, and then listened as he told me how the stress and strain of life as a London cabbie had affected the mental health of so many of his colleagues. At the same time, as it all poured out, I realised once again the simple presence of a dog like Max had allowed him to open up in a way that he might otherwise have kept bottled up.

By the time we caught the train out of London for the north, Angela and I flopped in our seats while Max sat happily under the table. We'd been so busy that I hadn't had a chance to check the Facebook page. I logged on, and then realised it would take me the entire journey back to Penrith to get through all the messages. Coverage of our Royal visit had indeed made that day's paper, as relayed to me by the cab driver, and that had been picked up by a whole host of media outlets. One newspaper had even celebrated Max's presence at the Royal Garden Party in their daily cartoon by poking fun at the fact that no cats had been invited. It was a delight and made the train trip pass quickly, but the one thing I wanted to see more than anything awaited our return … two, to be precise.

'Is that Kerry and Max? This pair have missed you!'

As soon as the door opened, just after I had knocked, both Paddy and Harry flew out to greet Angela and me. Such was their enthusiasm, I barely had a chance to say hello to the hostess and thank her for their stay. Instead, we all made our way to a field adjacent to the house so the three boys could reunite and let off steam. There, as we shared the highlights of our journey, I watched Max chase around with his apprentice, Paddy, and his little brother, and reminded myself that I was a very fortunate man indeed. I had Angela, who meant the world to me, and a family like no other in the form of three sweet, loyal and loving Spaniels.

This life had presented me with many challenges, right from the beginning, but with these dogs at my side, I had overcome it all and become more human for the experience.

Acknowledgements

I HAVE TO START by thanking my wife Angela, who supported me in those dark years, pushing me when I needed it. She saw me at my lowest point and never once complained when Max walked into our lives (although she might have complained about the hoovering he created). You make my world complete.

Max, there are no words that come close to describing our time together. The listener, the guide, the experience-maker, the light giver, the emotion, fun and laughter. Thank you for choosing me. I hope you've enjoyed the ride as much as I have.

To Paddy and Harry, for introducing us to the crazy world of just being more Spaniel (and a lot more hoovering).

Thanks to everyone at HarperCollins for their professionalism, patience and support during this project. Special thanks to Zoe, my editor, for making the call and encouraging me to tell my story. Your team have all been incredible to work with and I'll be forever grateful.

To Matt Whyman, for sitting, listening and putting words in place that tell our story so well. Congratulations on becoming a fellow Spaniel owner.

And for all those who came and walked and talked.

The UK's leading veterinary charity

PDSA is a lifeline for pets and owners, saving hundreds of thousands of pets' lives every year

To read more heart-warming stories visit **pdsa.org.uk/miraclemax**

Find us on

 @PDSA_HQ @PDSA @teampdsa /PDSAHQ